"This witty and thought provoking book makes ideal reading for students of the many courses available in management. The book outlines characters inhabiting what Shelley calls "the organizational zoo." People are characterized as various animals moving from A to Z. He shows great insight and wit, and one of the valuable features of this book is that, through the animal metaphor, he makes it easier for us to recognise some of the motivations of our coworkers, clients, and those we depend upon. My own perspective on this book is colored by my project management experience. I can see how viewing project stakeholders, as well as the many team members we interact with, as various animal species helps make sense of organizational cultures and a given situation's ethos. The book also has several appendices, one with a management game that can be both fun and instructive. I will be using this as a management text as well as recommending it as light reading."
> —Professor Derek Walker, Graduate School of Business,
> RMIT University, Melbourne

"A fresh approach to organizational culture development"
> —Steve Denning, author, *A Leader's Guide To Storytelling*,
> former Program Director, Knowledge Management, World Bank

"This book has tremendous potential to be used in all types of organizations, large and small. Having a tool that people can use to identify themselves or others in a nonthreatening way helps to break down many barriers that exist around cultural and behavioral issues. Hey, let loose and have some fun with it!"
> —Linda Page, Project Director, Knowledge Management,
> Strategic Management Division,
> Victorian Department of Treasury & Finance

"An excellent resource. In my 25 years consulting, I have been in many organizational zoos! Arthur's fun approach to understanding the personalities in the workplace is unique and engaging. Beware the animals."
> —Dr. Rod Dilnutt, Principle, William Bethwey and Associates

"*The Organizational Zoo* is a refreshing and highly entertaining contribution to the somber discipline of organizational behavior. For those wanting to enhance their self-awareness and find a humorous way to decipher the humanness around them, this book will provide the insight they are seeking. Having taught many of the creatures at a tertiary level, I now have validation that the truly successful ones were those who found their natural habitats."
> —Valerie Panayiotou, BAppSc, M.D.
> Organizational Effectiveness Consulting Pty Ltd

"Disarmingly simple; chillingly accurate;creates a compelling typology of business jungle inhabitants."
—Dr. Kate Andrews, Partner, Intellectual Capital, BDO Kendalls

"One of those thoroughly enjoyable books you can pick up at anytime, open anywhere and instantaneously relate to your working world."
—Graeme Allan, Director, Seifen Consulting Pty. Ltd.

"This book has something for everyone. For some it will be a lot of fun, while for others it will be a didactic window into the workings of organizations. Most of us at some time have played a private game of matching people we know with members of the animal kingdom. However, Arthur Shelley has very skillfully taken this game and applied it to an organizational setting. With this book, we can still play our little games, but the author has given us an excellent and expansive framework with which to play. From a bit of fun has come a very useful and insightful book for the workplace."
—Dr. Hilton Deeth, University of Queensland

"Read the book over the weekend and enjoyed it. Love those insects! And the difference between the Lion CEO and his Eagle counterpart. Also liked the way the book in the end was an exhortation for people to develop some self-knowledge. I suspect it will be a winner."
—Leon Gettler, business writer, *The Age* newspaper, Melbourne

"I can vividly imagine the whole thing coming together....how to successfully utilize each person's strengths to get a productive outcome. You don't try to change the natures of these beasts but rather accept them for who they've become or chosen to be, and then work within that paradigm."
—David Hyde, Business Consultant

"Have you ever thought, 'Man, this place is a zoo'? Well, you're certainly not alone. *The Organizational Zoo* is a deliciously witty and entertaining read that guides you through the dark forests and life forms that make up the zoo where you work. This biological metaphor has a serious side too. If we better understand each other and communicate more effectively, we can make our workplace a lot more fun.
—Mikael Hatzis, Managing Director, Integratos (and an Eagle)

"How often do we fail to take into account the highly variable human element when we seek to interact? *The Organizational Zoo* offers a fun way to do this, and to understand the way we interact by using metaphors from the animal kingdom that shed new light on our behaviors and styles in a short space of time. With simplicity, engagement and effect, I believe this book has enormous potential wherever the effective interaction of people is paramount."
—Frank Connolly, Victorian Public Service
Continuous Improvement Coordinator,State Services Authority

The Organizational Zoo

A Survival Guide to
Work Place Behavior

by

Arthur Shelley

Illustrations by John Szabo

Aslan
PUBLISHING

Fairfield, CT

Aslan Publishing
2490 Black Rock Turnpike, #342
Fairfield, CT 06825
Please contact the publisher for a free catalog.
Phone: **203/372-0300**
Fax: **203/374-4766**
www.aslanpublishing.com

Library of Congress Cataloging-in-Publication Data

Shelley, Arthur.
  The organizational zoo : a survival guide to work place behavior / by
Arthur Shelley ; illustrations by John Szabo.
      p. cm.
  Summary: "Compares individuals within organizations to ants, bees,
chameleons and other creatures from A to Z. By recognizing the secret
strengths and weaknesses of each animal and the animal nature of each co-
worker, the work world becomes more manageable. One can then build
teams with a productive mix of behaviors."—Provided by publisher.
  ISBN 0-944031-46-3 (alk. paper)
  1. Organizational behavior. 2. Interpersonal relations. 3. Adaptability
(Psychology) 4. Organizational effectiveness. I. Title. II. Title: Work place
behavior.

  HD58.7.S516 2006
  302.3'5—dc22
                                    2006022510

Editing by Marcia Yudkin
Book design by Dianne Schilling
Cover design by Miggs Burroughs
Printing by R.R. Donnelley, Inc.
Printed in the USA

To all who have been preyed upon and survived:
May your experiences continue to make you stronger, wiser and
better at reading the behaviors of those above you in the food chain.
and ...
To those about to begin your career safari:
Prepare well! Invest time with positive creatures and
ensure conflicts happen in your terrritory on your terms.

Foreword

This book consists of humorous observations of the characteristics and behaviors of the creatures in your "Organizational Zoo." It provides some essential survival guidelines for the safari that is your career. As you read, you will come to recognize the various Zoo creatures and learn how to deal with them. This book gives great insight for the inexperienced and provides a useful reinforcement reference for the more experienced among us who every day must manage the interactions between the creatures in our Zoos.

Disclaimer

No creatures were harmed in the making of this book, although some may be a little insulted at being compared to their human equivalents. Any apparent victimization or vilification of creatures is entirely coincidental and applies only to the stereotype, not to any individual creature.

Any creatures claiming to be adversely affected by the content of this book may submit a complaint in writing directly to the author. Any humans who can see themselves in any of the profiles are congratulated for being self-aware. If you don't like what you see, don't bug me about it. Do something about it yourself.

The characters in this book are indeed real, but their names have been suppressed to protect the innocent (me). If you think you recognize yourself, just remember we all have different perspectives (see Glossary), and I might not have meant you. If you are considering the possibility to sue me, I *definitely* did not mean you.

Acknowledgements

To my friends and like-minded work colleagues, on whom I have structured the positive creatures, thank you for saving my sanity by being there, to balance the zoo. You know who you are. I hope you recognize the creatures in whose personas I have depicted you.

To the others I have worked with and have painstakingly studied in order to survive, thank you for this developmental opportunity. You also know who you are, unless you have not yet figured out the difference between perspective and reality (see Glossary).

To Joy, my wife, and my "little creatures" Cathy and Helen at my home Zoo, thank you for your inspiration and support during the writing of this book.

To John, what can I say? Without your creativity and sense of humor this book would be just a bunch of words. The illustrations and the fun we had in generating the illustrations bring the whole Zoo concept to life. Many more people will have fun with the concept as a result of being better able to visualize the creatures in their Zoos. I expect some may have trouble looking their colleagues in the eyes once they have the creature image of them in their minds.

Several people have read this book in manuscript form and provided valued feedback (Joy, Cathy and Helen Shelley, John Szabo, Liz Szabo, Steven Denning, Lesley Kyle, Jenny Thomas, David Hyde, Kathryn Bundy, Mike Nelson, Prof. Derek Walker, Dr. Beverley Lloyd-Walker, George Goode, Nancy Cashman, Helen Goode and Yvonne Glover). Thanks for your efforts! I appreciate your assistance in making this book more readable and more entertaining for a wider readership.

Thanks to Frank Connolly and the Continuous Improvement Network for their ongoing interest in *The Organizational Zoo* and their involvement in testing some of the exercises.

The scientists and journalists who make creature behavior documentaries have played a significant part in influencing my thinking and may have been the original inspiration of this concept. From one thought springs another, even if it goes in a different direction. It is this diversity of thinking and application of thoughts to other fields that leads us to new concepts and continues our evolutionary journey.

Special thanks to Barbara Hoberman Levine for having faith in my work and risking this unusual project with an unknown author. I appreciate your guidance and support. Thanks also to Marcia Yudkin, Dianne Schilling and Miggs Burroughs for their excellent assistance in editing and design.

Contents

Organizational Zoo character summaries can be found at:
www.organizationalzoo.com

The Organizational Zoo Concept

The concept of the Organizational Zoo came to me while travelling to a meeting I dreaded. I did not wish to attend because of the combination of "creatures" that were going to be present, with no sheltering plants in sight. I imagined the range of managers who were going to be at the meeting and why they were gathering. It felt as if they were herding the prey on the open grasslands in order to execute their will.

This fleeting analogy stuck in my mind and slowly built into a wider metaphor that seemed to apply to the whole organization. I realized that viewing the organization metaphorically as a collection of creatures interacting in, and with, their environment was a useful analysis tool. It provided a removed perspective to assess relationships and the flow of interdependencies in the environment.

Using this approach, I reconsidered how to approach the meeting. It was going to be a feeding frenzy. The predators had arranged the gathering on their terms so the pickings would be easy and the prey plentiful. I had to devise a strategy of how to survive the meeting without being wounded by the predators. I could run away (a very useful creature tactic, which only delays the inevitable). I could just stand tall and take the punishment like a plant, simply regrowing the lost pieces after the frenzy. But why be dominated? There had to be something else that could be done. What would other creatures do to shift the situation back into their favor?

Fish, like plants, just accept that some are going to be eaten. Aggregating in large schools, they consider safety in numbers as the best survival strategy (until their own the number is up, of course). In effect, they stack a meeting to reduce the risk to any specific individual. However, Russian roulette never really appealed to me, especially when I am betting my own life.

Perhaps, like a rabid dog desperate for survival, I could attack anyone that came remotely close to me with great aggression. Maybe I could be a blue-ringed octopus and rapidly change the landscape by emitting an "ink screen" to distract the predators.

While thinking through how we could learn from how nature responds, it occurred to me that perhaps we have not evolved as far as we would like to think. There are many lessons that we could learn from nature, which could apply very well to the business world. The natural balance that exists in nature is something rarely achieved in human systems. Despite occasional disturbances across the food chain, from plants to herbivores to small and then large carnivores, nature usually rebalances herself. It is only when humans interfere that nature loses control and falls out of balance. Could we learn from nature how to better manage our systems?

Once we have arrived at the concept that we are just creatures in a wider, balanced environment, the metaphor quickly extends. What type of character am I? Am I just prey or something more noble like a plant? How can we work more in harmony with each other and the wider environment? How do we win the struggle to avoid extinction through the ravenous actions of a bunch of enthusiastic predators? ....The successful species make the world work for them rather than being dictated to by others.

First, figure out who's who in the Zoo. Then determine what to fight for and what to concede to keep the predators at bay. Very quickly, you can see how you can grow the metaphor for yourself, and have fun in the process. Who belongs in which species and how should we best deal with them? In this book, we present the common producers, predators and prey, to give you a leg up for your safari through your chosen Zoo.

So, when you next wander through the corridor, give a deep growl as you pass the lion or pat the dog on the head and see what reaction you get. Sit back and reflect on how the majestic oak was once but a mere acorn (perhaps a wayward nut just trying to survive). However, if it can germinate and survive from being a fragile sapling before becoming the robust inspiration it is today, imagine what you can become.

Be careful with a liberal use of metaphor, though, as you will be surprised to find that not everyone has a sense of humor! Metaphor branding can be misunderstood and turn into a dangerous game. Some people will perceive their type quite differently from how you see them. Sometimes they see themselves as completely opposite to how you see them and can misinterpret your intent in applying the "wrong" classification.

One more thing to be aware of before you start using these animal metaphors on your colleagues. Think about why they work. We all get a sense of recognition when we read profiles. Sometimes we chuckle at seeing ourselves and other times we laugh at others. Often we can see pieces of ourself in several different profiles. This recognition gives us a sense of belonging to something. Finding a sense of belonging with an identity is natural and helps us to relate to each other more easily. You commonly hear statements like, "Oh! So you're a Gemini, now I understand!" Or, "I can so tell that you were born in the year of the Ox!" Alternatively, "I see your Australian characteristics coming out there." (Not hard, of course, as these are somewhat strong tendencies!)

Identities and classification schemes make our life easier. They represent patterns that we can put people into, so we can quickly tell if we want to deal with them or not. The truth is, we are constantly subconsciously classifying people into stereotypical identities we have in our heads. We have to. Who the heck has the time for a detailed analysis of the personality of everyone you meet? Generally, assessment of others is completed in a few seconds. Something like... Hmm, seems like a nerd, babe, jock, boffin, bookworm, loser or "the one." Game over! You have been detected, inspected, reflected upon and rejected or accepted. Very rarely is a second chance given, for our intuition has spoken.

Once classified, you have been set into a given category, and contradictory signals received later are seen as you behaving a bit out of character. By the time you have finished your first sentence, your new acquaintance has already put you in a profile and decided whether to engage further or ignore you at the first opportunity. We call it instinct or intuition, but in reality our brain is doing some serious profile matching in our subconscious to pass judgement from these first impressions.

The trouble with this approach is that sometimes we read the signals incorrectly. Our poor tendency to classify people on immediate perceptions is one that humans could do with reducing to generate better assessments. We could learn from Nature on this. Nature takes her time in building relationships and keeps a good balanced approach.

Some plants have co-evolved with creatures to develop mutually beneficial relationships. Some have developed seeds that are consumed by the predator and deposited them later in a nice pile of... well, shall we say... fertilizer. This helps the plant spread and flourish in another location. Likewise, many plant and creature parasites inhabit their hosts and live off them, but not usually to the point that they kill them, except when they have a lifeline to the next host.

Nature recognizes how important it is to maintain the balance to keep the whole in flux. Humans have some difficulty in keeping the balance in their relationships. They often don't sufficiently understand who they are dealing with and how they can best relate to them for longer term success, especially in work environments. Too many relationships are one-sided and don't have sufficient consideration of longer term impacts on their partners.

Having better defined character profiles and a wider set of profiles helps us to understand others more and interact better with them. We still need to make our judgements and classifications based on our reading of signals, but we can do these from a more solid foundation and over a longer time. Some people are better at rapid assessments than others. Some read very accurately and quickly and are rarely wrong. Others, sadly, have strings of poor relationships because they don't have the right behavioral patterns in their brains to categorize correctly, or they receive the signals completely wrongly (or believe the lies they are being told).

The early signals you get from others are usually those your new acquaintance wants you to get. Also, your reading of them is biased by your own history. So, it is never as simple as you think.

As you proceed to measure others by this set of creature and plant profiles, always remember that what you see will always be different from what others see. The lion sees himself as a majestic beast who protects the pride. A mouse sees the lion as the aggressive set of teeth that just consumed his family for a light afternoon snack. The Oaks see themselves as essential providers of food and shelter, and as having a critical role in the nurture of the environmental balance. Many people see them as only being useful when they are reduced to timber and clearing the way for "development".

Just knowing the capabilities, tendencies and behaviors of the characters in your zoo, will place you in a better position for the future. Study those in your zoo over time to be sure you have them correctly classified. Understand their moods, inconsistencies and vagaries. Know their strengths and weaknesses and how to mange through these. Get to know them well and learn how to interrelate with them, on your terms, not theirs.

Benefits of Applying the Zoo Concept

Your Zoo will never be the same again after you have this concept in your mind. It will assist you to construct strategies on how to deal with difficult characters and relieve some of the stress by making this more of a game. Hopefully, it will assist in your development or your development of others. Remember, we work to live, not live to work. Have some fun thinking about the creatures in your Zoo.

You have several choices as to how to act on the contents of this book:

1. Be sensible and establish a structured safari on your own terms.

Understanding the creatures in the Zoo and your own characteristics provides you with great advantages. You can establish a strategy to deal with the other creatures and even manipulate your environment to maximize your own progress. We can learn how to develop into something more than just being energy content for larger predators. You may even decide that you can establish your own Zoo that contains only the creatures that are compatible with yourself.

2. Be less sensible and use the book only for entertainment.

You may be completely satisfied with your own characteristics and survival strategy and choose not to change anything. However, this does not mean that your reading time was wasted. Two reasons for this are:

(i) You had fun reading the book and now can have even more fun gossiping about management in terms that they may not understand, and

(ii) You have probably learned how to size up the competition better and confirmed your position in the Zoo.

You could even fantasize about which creature you want to transform into during your lunch break. Perhaps you can do this in meetings if you are bored and think you can get away with it. Most people will not notice, except when you really get into it and you give your game away through a distant look and huge grin.

3. Be highly intelligent and happy and do both 1 and 2.

This just proves that you are a highly evolved but still adaptable creature and are bound to do very well. With this perspective, you can probably survive in many Zoos and maintain a well-balanced life. We need more like you on this planet, ideally spread among many Zoos to assist them in becoming more balanced. Go forth and multiply!

4. Do nothing.

This prompts the question of why you even bothered to read this at all. Maybe just to waste some time over a lazy break? Unfortunately, the world is full of creatures who gather much information and then complain about it as nothing ever comes out of knowing it. They constantly miss the point that information is beneficial only when it is applied to create a difference, action or value.

If we want to improve our circumstances, we need to use the information we have to make better decisions and drive actions. We watch traffic in order to decide the best time to cross the road. However, watching and deciding do not get us across. Ultimately, life is about experience and experience is about doing something!

Part 1

Zoo Characters

Common Creatures in the Zoo

Like most large organizations, a Zoo is a very abnormal mix of creatures that do not naturally cohabit. In the Zoo, they reside in much closer proximity than they would in nature and this causes stress. In a more natural setting, outside the organization, they would either avoid each other, or if part of the same food chain, eat or be eaten by their colleagues. In a politically correct world, the rules of the organization should protect them from each other, but the rules do not usually govern. They only restrict what is allowed to be seen.

Predators roam the corridors and meeting rooms. They go on feeding frenzies and those lower in the food chain try to remain out of the way to survive. This book is about the characteristics of many of the species you are likely to experience during your career safari. Although each Zoo keeps a different collection of creatures on display, those listed here are the common ones that you are most likely to come across.

The creatures are portrayed as neither male nor female as it is possible for the characteristics to apply to either gender. In reality, the human equivalents of some creatures are more likely to be male or female. However, don't make the mistake of misjudging your creatures based on gender as you will get yourself into trouble quite quickly. (See Political Correctness in the Glossary.)

Equally, any of these creatures, or variations of them, can appear in any culture. Those who have worked in many parts of the world recognize the same creatures all over the place. They may observe slightly different sub-species, depending upon the niche that cultural environment provides, but nevertheless basically the same. The creature profiles included in this book have been thoroughly researched to provide a complete set of profiles that apply in most organizations.

Part I lists the most common types of creatures alphabetically and describes their characteristics and how to deal with them. In Part II, we view the Zoo as a whole and how the structure of the Zoo determines how well the creatures survive.

Alphabetical List of Zoo Character Profiles

 is for Ant

Characteristics:

Ants have a great work ethic and are great at teamwork. This is largely because they put the colony before the individual. They are extremely powerful in a physical sense in that they get through an enormous volume of menial tasks. They are an essential part of every ecosystem, taking other creatures' wastes and using it as food or to build their nests. Ants play an essential role in recycling resources back into the ecosystem in usable form.

You have to take some care with them because although they are selfless, this only extends to their own colony. They have little interest in other colonies and will assume they are enemies. They go into attack mode if they feel their own colony is being threatened, but are normally docile.

While individual ants will not achieve much on their own, collectively they can construct major engineering works in relatively short time spans. The underground network of tunnels that form the ant nest is an engineering marvel that serves as shelter, nursery, food storage and home to thousands of individuals.

Relating to the Ant:

Ants are simple basic workers and are found in every Zoo, even though they are not on exhibit. They work hard together in the background doing what needs to be done. They have a basic social structure that generates collaboration without much outside influence. Simple communications (chemical markers) from one ant to another drive others to react in a particular manner, like "build a nest here," "follow this trail to food," and so on.

You can influence what the ant does and where it does it by providing attractants, such as food or convenient shelter. They will naturally take advantage of these to enhance their environment, but they are not great planners as such. They just react to what comes. Provided you don't upset them by getting in the way of what they are doing, they will laboriously go about their construction and maintenance work.

Ants don't particularly like or dislike relating to other characters in the Zoo. They happily operate alongside most types until their activities are interfered with. Then they can become aggressive regardless of who the interfering party is.

Success for the Ant:

- Getting the required work done alongside their peers.
- Being left undisturbed while they get on with what needs to be done.

Attributes often applied to the Ant:

- Busy
- Hardworking
- Communal
- Loyal
- Dedicated
- Territorial
- Present Focused
- Instinctive

Attributes not often applied to Ants:

- Sensitive
- Self-aware
- Thinking
- Logical
- Decisive
- Individualistic
- Visionary
- Reflective

B is for Bee

Characteristics:

Bees are the ultimate team workers. They share what they know to ensure that all benefit, and they aggressively defend the team as a whole. Bees, like ants, have a great work ethic and communicate well. However, unlike ants, they have far more complex ways to use shared knowledge to drive what they do. Rather than just act instinctively, they plan ahead and have many ways to protect the hive and communicate what they know to others for the benefit of the whole hive. Bees use different dances to tell other bees where food is located and release pheromones (chemical scents) to pass on other messages, such as the alarm signal if the hive is under attack.

Bees use their knowledge to control the environment to suit their purposes, rather than simply reacting to what happens to them. By doing this, they see through difficult times. Bees do not hibernate over winter. They manage the internal temperature of the hive by limiting the openings and actively flapping their wings to generate heat. They create additional honey in the summer to provide their energy requirements during their "lean periods," in effect planning ahead. In summer they keep the hive cool by bringing water into the hive and allowing it to evaporate.

Bees have quite a complex social structure, with separation of duties for the Queen, Drones, and Workers. The workers are all female and their duties are further divided based on their age. Young bees clean cells and care for the young and the Queen. In middle age they build, ventilate and maintain the hive and store the honey. The more experienced worker bees forage for food. Drones are there solely for reproduction, and many are required to maintain genetic diversity, but they are evicted if food is in short supply.

Bees have complex forms of protection in addition to their stingers. They build a specially constructed single opening to the hive, which is guarded by special attendants. They build their nests in hard to access places. They add floral herbicides and fungicides to the internal walls of the hive. They produce biocides, which they add to the honey to protect it from microbial spoilage, and they have a colony-specific odor, which allows them to identify each other and any intruders.

Relating to the Bee:

Bees are normally highly cooperative creatures. They help out their own hive members and even willingly help out other types of creatures, providing there is a two-way relationship. Bees provide honey and wax for others to use, and in return for this they get their hives moved around to plentiful sources of pollen and water by their human keepers. However, if they feel that they are under attack or they continue to be "used" in a one-way relationship they can get very nasty indeed. They can mount a particularly intimidating, painful counterattack.

"Human Bees" naturally form networks of people who have similar interests and want to collaborate for the good of the whole community (and across communities). Treat them with some respect and give them something back, and bees can make your Zoo a much more productive environment.

Human bees are highly productive, both directly (creating honey) and indirectly (pollinating flowers). But unhappy bees are unproductive and aggressive. Happy human bees cross-fertilize a whole range of other projects in the environment as they go about their work.

Bees relate very well to other collaborative and hardworking character types such as ants, mice, owls and some dogs. They highly respect the *Quercus robur* and eagles but have an aversion to lions, hyenas and rattlesnakes.

Interestingly, bees don't think too much about themselves. They think more of the community and the role they play in it. Other creatures see bees as positive contributors but are generally wary of them because of their potential aggressiveness if their work is disturbed in any way.

Success for the Bee:

- Sharing knowledge with others so that maximum benefit can be generated for the entire community.
- The bee's ultimate success is the creation of a new colony by virtue of being successful enough to be able to support the development of a new Queen who will take over the existing hive (as the old Queen will migrate to a new location with enough loyal supporters to make a new hive).

- Short-term successes such as surviving another winter are not considered successes; they are just another step on a longer term successful journey.

Attributes often applied to the Bee:

- Busy
- Hardworking
- Collaborative
- Communicative
- Communal
- Sociable
- Organized
- Territorial
- Intelligent
- Knowledgeable
- Loyal
- Caring
- Aggressive (when threatened)

Attributes not often applied to Bees:

- Self-aware
- Individualistic
- Gullible
- Political
- Slow
- Reflective

C is for Chameleon

Characteristics:

Chameleons are masters of disguise. They change their appearance and actions on a whim depending upon their environment. They quickly adopt the colors of the environment as the environment changes but do not change the environment. Their key defense is to look and behave the same as where they are by becoming virtually invisible.

These creatures also have an ingenious curling tail, which allows them to manipulate themselves out of difficult situations. This is complemented by a rapid-fire tongue, which they use to ambush unsuspecting small prey as it passes by.

It is interesting that chameleons do not survive in captivity very well. They tend to stress as they cannot adapt well in strange circumstances and are unable to manipulate the environment to suit their own cause.

Relating to the Chameleon:

Chameleons are dangerous in that they always adjust their reaction to align with whomever they are with, thus making them unreliable. They agree with you and then say the opposite when with someone else who has a different opinion. While unreliable, they are predictable if you know whom they will be with. They usually get themselves into trouble in mixed company, not knowing which side to align with if differences are raised in the discussion.

In human organizations, chameleons are the "Yes people." They tend to align themselves with more than one management network. In case they fall out with one, they have other backup relationships. Chameleons are not brave enough to make decisions of major importance. They can be dangerous because they reinforce the arguments being proposed by someone important, regardless of it being right or wrong (because they just want to agree). However, in doing this they give the proposal greater credibility.

You can use a chameleon as a conduit to a decision maker. If you explain your proposal to them, they will inevitably agree with you, so you may be able to encourage them subtly to discuss it with a key decision maker to get some initial feedback. If the decision maker does not like it, the chameleon will of course agree with them. Nevertheless, you can find out from the chameleon what it is the decision maker did not like and adjust it accordingly if this is appropriate.

I always prefer to talk things through with the decision maker, but when this is not possible a chameleon can provide an opening. The process of the deliberate political leak is something like this mechanism — let it out and if popular, take credit; if unpopular, deny it was ever being considered (or it was only a suggestion that was discussed and rejected).

Chameleons try to relate to everyone, changing their colors to blend in with whom they are with. They are often inappropriately adopted by others, because they don't create contrary opinions of their own and because they appear to support those around them. They appeal to characters with egos, reinforcing their self-esteem.

Chameleons see themselves as the peacemakers of the world. They think that by agreeing with everyone, they somehow make differences disappear. The reverse is usually true: People get confused, disappointed or angry when they hear different messages from the same source. Others see chameleons, once they know their true colors, as deceiving liars, but may try to use this in constructive ways.

Success for the Chameleon:

- Being accepted by important people and being seen to be so by others.
- Disappearing by blending back into the environment when things go wrong.
- Being actively engaged in both sides of an argument and appearing to be in support of each of the opposing parties.

Attributes often applied to the Chameleon:

- Two-faced
- Cunning
- Manipulative
- Weak
- Political
- Intelligent

Attributes not often applied to Chameleons:

- Loyal
- Trustworthy
- Consistent
- Confident
- Challenging
- Action-oriented

# D is for Dog

Characteristics:

Dogs are a highly versatile and enthusiastic group of creatures—loyal followers, not leaders. The ultimate behavior of any individual dog is highly dependent upon who their master (leader) is and their environment. A young pup is playful and highly gullible. They will do anything to please the master and don't challenge the correctness of what they are taught. They learn fast, but find it difficult to unlearn bad habits and reform into new habits. This explains why dogs have such a wide range of roles in the Zoo, from lap dogs, tracker dogs and guide dogs to guard dogs, attack dogs and hunting dogs.

While there are variations in aggressiveness and intelligence among pups, their ultimate behavior patterns are more influenced by their training and mentoring than by their inherent characteristics. You can get a vicious little lap dog just as easily as you can get a docile dog almost the size of a horse.

Relating to the Dog:

Dogs can learn anything and will do so enthusiastically, as long as you provide the discipline and reward system and you are consistent in applying it. Left without training, they can do all sorts of random damage. Trained correctly, they can perform acts of highly specific damage or they can perform acts of great good and prevent damage being done. In short, train your dog to do what you want to be done. Feed it well and it will serve you very loyally for a long time without challenging what it is you are asking it to do.

One point of caution with dogs: While we think we know them well and can trust them completely, they occasionally do the unpredictable. Stories of a dog biting for no apparent reason are common. Even the loyal family pet has been known to have an uncharacteristically bad day and savage either a family member or a friend. Their creature instincts simply lash out from beneath their refined behavior and can cause serious damage. So we love and trust our dogs, but there should always be a little caution in the back of our minds.

Many people start their careers as pups. They learn highly developed characteristics and capabilities and remain loyal and subservient to their master for life. Some go through a series of transformations to become quite a different dog, due to extreme stress or changed environmental circumstances. In rare cases they can go through an evolutionary transformation and behave very much like other creatures with which they associate. Dogs relate to all types, but like to be led. An attack dog develops if mentored by a vulture or a lion and a guide dog is created through close positive association with an owl or *Quercus* (providing they do not succumb to the temptation to do what dogs naturally do, when a tree appears).

Dogs see themselves as loyal and fun-loving. Others see dogs as fun, but perhaps sometimes misguided in their blind faith for their leaders. They usually avoid mature aggressive dogs belonging to other masters, believing in the old adage, "You can't teach an old dog new tricks."

Success for the Dog:

- Pleasing the master, especially their own master, but also other masters.
- Doing a trick well while more than one master is watching. A pat on the back is always welcome, along with a token treat.
- Being top dog of the pack is also a favored position where there are many dogs who interact regularly. A dogfight can occur where a group of dogs have not yet established who is who in the hierarchy. This is where the natural aggression of some dogs shows, especially if this has been encouraged by their master.

Attributes often applied to the Dog:

- Loyal
- Trusting
- Energetic
- Enthusiastic
- Boisterous
- Gullible
- Reliable
- Predictable
- Happy
- Playful
- Productive (when directed)
- Trustworthy (mainly)

Attributes not often applied to Dogs:

- Careful
- Serious
- Reflective
- Thinking
- Streetwise (for pups)

E is for Eagle

Characteristics:

Eagles are inspirational leaders. These magnificent creatures are, unfortunately endangered, because they are being out-competed by less scrupulous creatures. They have fantastic clarity of vision and can see very long distances. They know what they want and soar well above the rest of the Zoo. When they spy what they desire they grab the opportunity with great speed, accuracy and grace and return to great heights to enjoy their spoils.

Eagles are at the top of the food chain in their environment, despite the presence of much larger and physically stronger creatures. Their capabilities and behaviors enable them to avoid any dangers these larger creatures may pose, so they do not have to compete directly with them. They avoid the other powerful creatures in the environment because they have the ability to soar above them. From their great height and with their vision, they are more aware of the potential opportunities and risks and capable of reacting to them faster and more effectively.

Relating to the Eagle:

The eagle should be treated with great respect. They are powerful and extremely capable. They use their great vision and strong talons to quickly take advantage of any opportunity that arises. You can learn a lot about how to behave by observing them closely. Many cultures see them as epitomizing management behaviors and hold them in great esteem. Eagles demonstrate the importance of a high-level or long-term perspective and how to monitor the entire landscape.

Eagles relate well to other characters they consider competent and who have passion for what they do. They especially appreciate whales, bees and owls and are inspired by the *Quercus*. They dislike characters who are lazy or untrustworthy. They see a niche for aggressive types like the lions and hyenas, where aggressiveness can be put to good use. They do not understand how creatures like the sloth, snail and nematode justify their existence, other than by being fair game for the hungry.

Eagles see themselves as capable, energetic and justifiably on top of the food chain. They are confident in their abilities without being ungracious. Others generally see eagles with the respect they deserve, although sometimes lions envy them, not understanding why they are respected so highly. After all, they don't even have a pride to lord over!

Success for the Eagle:

- Passionate pursuit and achievement of success for the organization and themselves (and being recognized as doing so).
- Being considered by other eagles as being a great leader, since the opinion of other eagles matters more than anything else.

Attributes often applied to the Eagle:

- Intelligent
- Visionary
- Strong
- Focused
- Inspiring
- Confident
- Productive
- Decisive
- Balanced
- Sharp
- Action oriented
- Open
- Trustworthy
- Intuitive
- Aggressive
- Accountable
- Holistic
- Extroverted
- Respected

Attributes not often applied to Eagles:

- Procrastinating
- Emotional
- Weak
- Reclusive
- Shy
- Slow

F is for Feline

Characteristics:

Felines are highly independent and very capable creatures. They have great confidence in their own abilities and do not like to rely upon others. They are quite territorial and react violently to another feline in their territory (unless they are of the opposite gender and it is mating season). They have a nasty bite, savage claws and extreme agility with lightning-fast reflexes. Felines can be very dangerous if you are likely prey, considered an unwelcome intruder or a fluffy bunny that may be fun to chase.

They have a sinister side as well. Felines often capture prey and keep them alive to be used as practice to hone their hunting reflexes. There is no thought at all about the cruelty to the victim. It is all about how well they perform and whether they have improved their capabilities, or just for fun. Despite these formidable fighting capabilities, felines are cautious and not at all brave. They could easily inflict great damage to a dog or other much larger creature, but they rarely engage in such conflicts. While they may hunt small creatures just for fun, they quickly run away from any fairer contest. They stand and fight larger creatures only when absolutely forced to do so.

Felines spend a lot of time in self-grooming and like to ensure that they get lots of beauty sleep. They can become very fond of a few others, primarily those providing their main source of food and shelter but are otherwise quite antisocial. For those special few who have the privilege of serving them, felines go out of their way to show off their capabilities by bringing in a freshly killed mouse or bird. Such behavior is targeted at earning praise from their owner for being useful as well as a way of showing off their abilities. By bringing in their kill, they attempt to justify their aloof superiority.

Relating to the Feline:

Felines love to be admired and hate to be laughed at. Their daydream thoughts focus on how they were worshiped in ancient Egypt. Their vanity is their weak point, and they can become quite insulted if you embarrass them. But beware: they can inflict deep and severe wounds when they wish to.

Felines don't have a great deal of time for the opinions of others (purr-furing their own opinion). As a result, they don't bother relating to others much, although they secretly admire the majesty and agility of the lion. Some actually see themselves as a lion and desperately desire to have their power and status.

Other creatures see the feline as being distant and aloof but generally harmless. However, they are often wary of felines, as they have a tendency to hide and suddenly pounce without warning just for a bit of hunt practice.

Success for the Feline:

- Receiving an award and believing that others admire them.
- Showing off their highly tuned skills.

Attributes often applied to the Feline:

- Individualistic
- Agile
- Aloof
- Self-interested
- Vain
- Selfish
- Frustrating
- Arrogant

Attributes not often applied to Felines:

- Sociable
- Friendly
- Communal
- Caring
- Interesting
- Collaborative

G is for Gibbon

Characteristics:

Gibbons are the social fabric of the Zoo. Everyone loves to watch their antics, and they love to show off to a crowd. They don't do much else in the Zoo, but this frivolity and constant stream of entertainment is a positive contribution in its own right. They can be especially good at disarming stressful situations by adjusting the topic at hand or providing an alternative positive spin.

Gibbons can become very unhappy in situations where they do not have the freedom or time to express their social instincts. Under such circumstances they can become very rebellious and deliberately create mischief.

Relating to the Gibbon:

Gibbons actively seek your attention and are fun to be around. They perform best to a small captive crowd, like the Zoo party. Give them sufficient rope and they will weave some magic that brings people together and gets them working well as a team. Do not expect the gibbon to contribute greatly to the actual work delivery. They achieve through the improved morale and heightened productivity of others by positive influence. Do not make them head of a large project team, or nothing will ever get done. They serve best when they can be the creative force behind a leader who can then put the ideas into practice, or in roles like the office social club secretary or the events manager.

Gibbons are like chameleons in that they try hard to relate to everyone. The difference is that the gibbon truly wants to be everyone's friend and have fun with them. They like to play and don't understand why working life should be dreary and dull.

This sense of fun and "look-at-me" factor can have a negative impact on some other types, especially the feline who believes the gibbon has no credibility or worthy skills. Much of this is just jealousy on the part of the feline who thinks they deserve the public accolades. Lions, hyenas and many others are highly amused by the gibbon and enjoy watching their antics. However, when the pressure is on and performance is more important than play, the others lose patience with them.

Gibbons know they are the life of the party! They have absolute confidence that everyone has more fun if they are there, so why disappoint everyone? Some other creatures see the gibbon as a social animal that they don't rely upon too much unless it involves organizing social events, but this is a bit harsh as gibbons are more useful than this would imply.

Success for the Gibbon:

- Maintaining a wide network of friends and motivating others to complete tasks for social events.
- Being the main attraction and source of amusement at the annual office party.

Attributes often applied to the Gibbon:

- Happy
- Playful
- Energetic
- Enthusiastic
- Highly sociable
- Fun
- Interesting
- Cool
- Rebellious (if stressed)

Attributes not often applied to Gibbons:

- Careful
- Serious
- Productive
- Forward thinking
- Focused

H is for Hyena

Characteristics:

Hyenas are pack hunters who do not have the power to kill a large healthy beast. Instead, they gang up on weaker individuals and collectively overpower them. A single hyena can be a formidable enemy, but their real strength is through their collaboration with others. They are quite selective in who to collaborate with and who to attack and also about where this should happen and when. They are cunning, scheming and often quite political in the way they go about their business. They play as hard as they work and have a lot of rough fun together. Their raucous laughter can often be heard well into the evening after a hard day at the zoo.

They differ from the piranhas because piranhas immediately launch an attack whenever and wherever a potential opportunity arises, without any planning and collaboration. The hyena gang hunt is far better prepared. Before the ambush, they have ensured that they have the upper hand. Consequently, hyenas have a higher effectivity rate than piranhas.

Hyenas resemble lions in the way they hunt, but differ because they lack the sheer power and speed the lions have. As a result, they are lower in the food chain. They are not too proud to scavenge or steal the prey of another beast, if they can intimidate them through numbers. In the hyena gang, there is relative equality across the group. Members communicate with each other using markers they leave on plants in their territory. This also serves to ward off members of other gangs.

Relating to the Hyena:

Provided you are well prepared and in good condition, the hyena gangs should not be a threat. However, they are always watching, and if you give them the chance to ambush you, they will take it. You should observe them for your own safety and generally keep away from them if you can.

Hyena gangs build up around ambitious individuals who have been working together and among whom there is mutual trust. Their alignment has developed more through common traits and mutual enemies than any true mutual respect. Some hyenas have been known to change gangs, but this does not normally work out in the long term. The deviate hyena generally gets shunned by members of both gangs as they have severed the relationships forged in the first gang and are not trusted by the new gang. They become outcasts.

Hyenas see themselves as productive collaborators who often get a lot of the unpopular work done (such as removing the incapable creatures from the Zoo). In organizations, hyenas are used as aggressive workhorses to get jobs done, especially by lions. The hyena's aggression and tendency of the gangs to ambush others in trouble means that other characters don't often forge close relationships with hyenas.

Success for the Hyena:

- A successful ambush with enough food for the whole gang.
- Being a dominant gang member.

Attributes often applied to the Hyena:

- Aggressive
- Scheming
- Controlling
- Manipulative
- Strong
- Political (Territorial)
- Communal
- Opportunistic.

Attributes not often applied to Hyenas:

- Trustworthy
- Caring
- Considerate
- Tolerant
- Shy

I is for Insect

Characteristics:

Insects come in many varieties but can loosely be categorised into two types; the rare beneficial type and the ubiquitous pestiferous type that Pandora should never have let out of the box.

The beneficial insect facilitates cross-pollination and can generate a wealth of new opportunities and value. While some insects already mentioned, like the bee and the ant, are positive creatures, they largely assist others without knowing they have done so. The beneficial insect I refer to here is a more advanced version of these.

Some cross-pollinating insects build a highly specific mutually beneficial relationship with a specific plant. For example, the female Yucca moth lays her eggs in the Yucca plant flowers, where the caterpillar larvae live in the developing ovary and eat Yucca seeds. The Yucca flowers have co-evolved with the Yucca moth and are specifically shaped so that only this tiny moth can pollinate them. Both parties win from the relationship. The moth ensures genetic diversity for the plant, and the plant provides exclusive food, shelter and accommodation for the moth's offspring.

Unfortunately, the insect type most frequently encountered is not the beneficial type. The one we are all more familiar with is the unwanted pest, who flies or crawls in from outside the Zoo and consumes resources without being invited or wanted. These insects are extremely ravenous and multiply very rapidly if uncontrolled. Pestiferous insects include the negative swarming types of insects like locusts, mosquitoes and cockroaches.

Relating to the Insect:

Insects can be put to good use, provided you ensure that you select the right one for your purpose. You must be in control of them and manage their activities to your agenda. If you have selected well and have a beneficial type, your harvest can be greatly enhanced and they will be worth every effort you put into them.

However, if you have the wrong type and allow them to manage to their own agenda, they will quickly find ways to consume all of the resources you have. When resources are abundant, they quickly attract many additional insects to consume as much as possible and as quickly as possible. Once all of the available resources have been consumed, they will all swarm to the next pasture. They leave your Zoo greatly depleted and often worse off than when they arrived. It is unlikely that you will have received what they originally promised to deliver for you and highly likely that it will take a lot of work to bring your Zoo back to where it was before they arrived.

The common swarming varieties of insects are very difficult to control. Today you have one, tomorrow dozens, next week hundreds. Where insects have been put to the best use, it is where they have been used as a biological control against more pestiferous varieties of insects. For example, you can engage mantis varieties to exterminate (or at least control) the other swarms that have infiltrated your Zoo.

In the organizational world, beneficial insects can be found as members of small consultancies, industry bodies or external advisors who have your interests at heart. They focus on applying their knowledge to enhance your opportunities and wealth (and of course, for this they are justifiably rewarded handsomely). There is always a win-win relationship from them, and they assist periodically rather than attempt to create a dependency to ensure a long-term revenue stream from you (as pestiferous types do).

Pestiferous insects can be found wherever there are resources to be exploited. These self-interested consultants, advisors or management product retailers give the good insects a bad name. They are eager to "help" you through your crisis (even if you don't have one). They focus on how much value they can extract from you, before they consider what you get in return.

Beneficial insects are proud of what they are and what they do. They put great thought into where they can generate benefit and then get on and do it. Pestiferous insects are proud of what they can get out of what they do. They twitter to each other about the latest things they have and where the productive fields are. Others don't often see a true beneficial insect, but when they do they try to forge a long standing relationship with it. However, being bitten once by a pestiferous insect is usually too much and most would prefer never to see a swarm again.

Success for the Insect:

- Beneficial insects: Assisting you to get more from existing opportunities or generating new opportunities for you (while remaining independent, being respected and well rewarded for their services).
- Pestiferous insects: Consumption of all available resources before moving on to other tasty fields.

Attributes often applied to the Insect:

Beneficial Insects
- Beneficial
- Resourceful
- Helpful
- Positive
- Forward thinking

Pestiferous insects

- Arrogant
- Ubiquitous
- Ravenous
- Self-interested
- Swarming
- Costly

Attributes not often applied to Insects:

Beneficial Insects
- Selfish
- Arrogant

Pestiferous insects
- Caring
- Productive
- Beneficial

J is for Jackal

Characteristics:

Jackals are social animals who collaborate in small family groups to which they are very loyal. Agile hunters, they aggressively protect their territory. They are resourceful creatures and are often found in association with larger predators, as they can benefit from their kills. Pack members stay in touch through regular yipping calls, but they ignore the calls of those outside their pack. They protect the pack members when other jackals are away and share the load in busy times.

Elegant and well adapted to their environment, jackals have an almost dichotomous behavioral type, being friendly and dedicated to those in their group but often aggressive to outsiders. They cluster in cliques and exchange ideas and stories of attempted infiltrations to the group to learn from each other. Their sleek features and outwardly immaculate behaviors often camouflage their real strength, which lies in guarding. If you cross them, you will rapidly encounter their agile pounce and extremely sharp teeth.

Relating to the Jackal:

Jackals respond positively to genuine interest in them and in their clan. They react aggressively to being patronized or attempts to bypass them to get to their keepers. However, if you really want to fire them up, ignore them or downplay their importance. To get access to the pack, you need to foster a genuine relationship with the jackal over time. This requires regular visits and showing them that you appreciate them. The occasional visit to the jackal themselves when you do not need to get to the manager they are protecting will pay off handsomely. They believe in reciprocity and the importance of relationships. Genuine interest in them will boost your chances of keeper access when you really need to do business at short notice.

Jackals often can be found in support and protection roles. A key task of many jackals is to prevent the entry to uninvited guests to the senior managers of the Zoo. In an aggressive environment they can become political and overzealous, even.

Jackals relate well to all who are worthy of their time, and this entirely depends upon your social status, your relevance to them and your intentions. If you are not considered worthy, you will be ignored, unless you attempt to infiltrate the protected territory, in which case you will be warned. If you persist, you will be savagely attacked.

Jackals see themselves as the protectors of the Zoo's upper echelon. They exist to make their leaders' lives easier and to ensure they are not interrupted (and they generally are quite good at that). Others have varied views of the jackals, depending upon their experiences and their relationship with the jackals' leaders.

Success for the Jackal:

- Managing the affairs of the pack and the leaders and rejecting all but genuinely needed visitors.
- Being in control, especially controlling others higher in the food chain.
- Jackals love to gather in packs and exchange ideas and stories of their accomplishments. They like to be considered as effective, elegant, important and strong.

Attributes often applied to the Jackal:

- Highly territorial
- Zealous
- Social
- Aggressive
- Agile
- Controlling
- Jealous
- Fun loving (among their own group)
- Loyal (to their immediate clan)
- Caring (of those whom they consider worthy)

Attributes not often applied to Jackals:

- Patient
- Tolerant
- Shy
- Caring (of those they consider unworthy of their attention)

 is for Kid

Characteristics:

Kids are those small, cute and naive baby goats that everyone wants to hug, but who do not have much else to offer. They have no experience and spend their whole day bouncing about with great enthusiasm. Kids require constant direction from their elders to remain safe. They don't seem to understand danger, and many get themselves into dangerous predicaments through sheer ignorance. They learn through play with other kids and observation of their seniors. However, when they attempt to interact with or play with the seniors, they are not tolerated and are quickly put back in their place. They are constantly reminded that they have a lot of maturing to do before they become worthy of full membership in the herd.

Their human equivalent is the "new kid on the block," like the graduate recruit. Extremely vulnerable, they service the organization in basic functions. Organizations need a constant flow of new kids, but only a few remain in the Zoo long enough to transform into something greater. With the right development and mentoring, kids can mature and transform (see Transformation in the Glossary) into a more significant player, such as an owl or whale.

Relating to the Kid:

Kids need to be mentored in order to develop, contribute and prosper. Unfortunately, they are often taken advantage of or even sacrificed for the benefit of others (or in some organizations, just for sport). Their naive innocence allows them to be easily taken advantage of by the other creatures in the Zoo. If they are lucky they will hit on the right environment and be cared for by an owl or whale. Otherwise there is little hope for them.

Kids can be found in all organizations in basic roles such as apprentice, intern or office go-fer. They are often naive enough to believe the system will look after them.

Kids can relate to anyone as their wide-eyed innocence holds a nostalgic humorous interest for the more experienced creatures in the Zoo.

Some members feel they need to protect them and help them prosper, while others use them simply as a resource (or food, in some cases).

Kids who are lucky enough to relate to the right characters are rewarded with learning opportunities in a relatively safe environment from which they learn and grow.

Most kids are pragmatic enough to know they are at the bottom of the organizational ladder and accept this status for some time. However, with the advent of Generation Y, more are beginning to believe that there is no justification for this. Their expectations of advancement and opportunities are much higher than Generation X's, and their level of patience is lower. Other creatures have traditionally seen kids as the source of harmless fun and as a cheap resource to be used for menial tasks. However, now with increased political correctness, shorter tenure (higher turnover) of junior staff and greater expectations, the kid has lost some of that cute charm for some members of the Zoo.

Success for the Kid:

- Surviving long enough to go on to something else.
- Being noticed for achieving something positive or being cared for by a positive mentor who helps them to become more streetwise before it is too late for them.

Attributes often applied to the Kid:

- Naive
- Playful
- Energetic
- Enthusiastic
- Motivated (but without direction)
- Expendable
- Youthful

Attributes not often applied to Kids:

- Experienced
- Reliable
- Knowledgeable
- T ough
- Streetwise

 is for Lion

Characteristics:

Lions are aggressive and powerful leaders. They rule the pride with an iron paw and immediately and aggressively ward off any challengers. They protect their pride with energy and vigor. In return, all in the pride are subservient to the lion.

Lions declare themselves king of the Zoo, but this is not always reality. They usually just reign as the temporary king of their pride. Challengers are always waiting in the wings in this highly competitive environment. The balance of power is always at risk, being maintained by fear and physical strength. On the day the lion appears vulnerable, a succession challenge is likely. A more youthful lion, if successful, will then rule in the same way until the cycle repeats itself. The first thing a new king does is eat the younger male members of the newly conquered pride to ensure that their own reign lasts longer.

Young male offspring are tolerated in the pride only until they start to become strong enough to be a threat to the lion. They are ejected before they have the confidence to attempt a challenge. These young lions then roam alone or with siblings looking to be new kings in the pride of an aging lion.

As the king, they have others (primarily the lionesses) do much of the hard work for them, but the lion will always feast on a kill first while the rest of the pride wait to feed on the leftovers.

Relating to the Lion:

The lion is a force to be reckoned with. They are powerful, fast and agile beasts very aggressive if you are in their territory. They have a small army of loyal pride members they can rely upon to ambush you, and they will not hesitate to do so. This is not out of cruelty. It is just daily business to them, and they do it very well. They are not interested in outsiders joining their pride. They prefer to develop their own members from within.

Be wary of lions and always know where they are and what they are up to (even if you are one yourself). Never put yourself in a vulnerable position with them. If you happen to be unlucky enough to get landed into such a position, prepare as best as you can for an attack and get your sorry butt out of there as quickly as possible.

Lions are great to have in the right places in your Zoo, but they can also be dangerous. In the competitive corporate world, they are essential to fend off challenges from competitors and to command respect from your commercial teams. You just need to be sure they understand who the real competitors are. They sometimes spend more time competing with other lions within your own Zoo, than they do attacking lions from elsewhere.

Lions see themselves as powerful fearful creatures and so do most other creatures around them.

Success for the Lion:

• Being in charge and feared.
• Defeating a challenger.

Attributes often applied to the Lion:

• Strong
• Powerful
• Aggressive
• Controlling
• Lazy
• Self-interested
• Territorial
• Manipulative
• Confident

Attributes not often applied to Lions:

• Dedicated
• Hardworking
• Caring
• Shy

M is for Mouse

Characteristics:

Mice are not often seen, but we all know they are there behind the scenes scurrying about doing what needs to be done. Like ants, they do not overevaluate, they just get on with the work required quickly and efficiently. They differ from ants by being individualistic and not physically strong. Unlike ants, they perform the whole task themselves and they do it with little cooperation from others (and generally without being noticed by others, unless they do not complete their work).

As we know, the natural enemy of the mouse is the feline, although they can fall prey to a wide variety of larger carnivores. The felines make a point of wandering through the Zoo (when they can pull themselves away from their grooming) looking for mice to intimidate. They are not necessarily even hungry. They just enjoy the feeling of superiority they get when they prove they can generate fear in the smaller beasts. A nice game when the cards are stacked in your favor! Mice are quick learners and react to this by hiding and remaining out of sight when the feline is about. But when the feline is away, the mice do play (and work) hard.

Relating to the Mouse:

Mice don't need much supervision. They are capable of keeping themselves busy. The trick is to keep sufficient productive work in front of them. If mice finish what is required, they will happily occupy themselves with other work, even tasks that are not important. They just can't sit still. If there is nothing at all for them to do, they will become bored and this can lead to destructive behaviors, like shredding records, simply because they can and it is fun.

Mice tend to shy away from developing strong alliances with other character types. They don't feel the need to mingle with the "in group" or waste time on idle gossip. They are happy dealing within their own mice networks. They mostly fear felines, hyenas and the lions.

Mice see themselves as harmless productive family-oriented creatures who prefer to mind their own business. Other creatures see mice in a similar way, if they happen to encounter them. They don't think about them much, preferring to just leave them to their own devices.

Success for the Mouse:

- Getting the job done and being left alone.
- Surviving without being preyed upon.

Attributes often applied to the Mouse:

- Agile
- Enthusiastic
- Adaptable
- Productive
- Invisible
- Busy
- Individualistic
- Intelligent
- Economical
- Reliable

Attributes not often applied to Mice:

- Lazy
- Extroverted
- Self-centered
- Aggressive

N is for Nematode

Characteristics:

Nematodes are parasitic flatworms. Their only aim in life is to get through their lifecycle and infect the next Zoo. They are invisible to the naked eye, which is their main form of defense. This makes discovering those hidden among the spaghetti in the picture to the left somewhat of a challenge!

Nematodes take everything they need from their hosts, and they don't mind too much who the host is. For this pleasure, they contribute nothing in return. They are not normally fatal, as this would only prevent them from achieving their aims, but they can take sufficient nutrients from the host to damage the host's general health.

Nematodes spread through poor hygiene practices and can build up to high levels in a poorly managed environment. Every Zoo needs the occasional cleanout treatment to rid themselves of nematodes. However, such treatments are often not specific enough, causing a lot of other desired creatures to get lost in the process. (Corporate restructuring experts refer to this as collateral damage.) After a well-targeted nematode purge, the overall health of the Zoo improves as the inefficiencies in the system are reduced. However, a significant rebuild program may be required if the collateral damage has cleared out too much long-term corporate memory. Lost tacit knowledge can be very hard to replace.

In organizations, nematodes are those who simply park their brains at the gate and work for the money, rather than contributing to the success of the Zoo. This differs from ants, who work at a low level but actively want to contribute and are proud of their Zoo. Whereas ants feel part of the Zoo community, nematodes see it simply as a food source.

Relating to the Nematode:

Nematodes actively attempt to shun any limelight to avoid the possibility of being detected. As a result, they don't develop a relationship with any other creature except to parasitize them. They prefer to quietly drain the energy from all creatures in the host Zoo.

The best way to manage nematodes is to prevent their buildup with clean, good practices. If the Zoo is managed well, you can prevent nematode infections and get rid of the occasional infiltrator to hold off a major cleanout program.

Nematodes don't see themselves in any special way, and in fact they don't have eyes to see or a brain to think with. They just exist. Most other creatures don't see them either, mainly because they are so small and well hidden. But if they did, they wouldn't like them.

Success for the Nematode:

- Surviving on the proceeds of others without adding anything.
- Infecting other creatures and new Zoos.

Attributes often applied to the Nematode:

- Lazy
- Parasitic
- Dependent
- Self-centered
- Invisible

Attributes not often applied to Nematodes:

- Productive
- Friendly
- Considerate
- Communal

 **is for Owl**

Characteristics:

The owl is the eternal mentor. They resemble whales but are more versatile, more mobile and less prone to mistakes and accidents. Owls can survive well enough as independent individuals, but they prefer to take others under their wing to protect them and develop their capabilities.

Owls have a great knowledge, a fine sense of the environment and the behaviors of the creatures within their immediate environment. They have adapted to being kept in the dark by developing very keen hearing when their good eyesight cannot be used. Owls have been proven to be able to catch prey completely in the dark by sound alone. They have learned to monitor a range of signals in order to get the optimal outcome. Despite being very capable predators, they are not outwardly aggressive. They know when to pounce and when to silently wait. They use logic, intelligence and strategy to manage their own affairs and to assist others whom they trust and respect.

Relating to the Owl:

The owl should be respected and approached when you think they can be of assistance. Generally they are willing to help if they can and if they believe your purpose to be honorable. They may show a wise reluctance to contribute when they know their best advice will not be taken or used appropriately. They know how others are likely to misuse advice to inappropriately manage a situation. In such circumstances, they may remain as a hidden advisor in the background, but not actively engaged in the program.

Owls take it upon themselves to mentor others. They carefully self-select candidates they believe are worthy of their investment. However, the Zoo benefits by providing some formality around owl mentoring activities. This increases the beneficiaries and the impacts of the mentoring.

Many owls are long-term (although not necessarily senior) employees who have a wide set of experiences and who have a collaborative attitude. They actually like to contribute. They understand that the Zoo improves when they can educate others and have more people working more productively. They know that the power of knowledge comes from sharing it to multiply its effects. Creatures less wise than the owl try to keep knowledge to themselves, thinking this makes them more valuable and more powerful. However, they fail to realize that this means they will always be bound to the role they currently have, unable to move on to something better.

Owls see themselves, and are seen by others, as respected mentors.

Success for the Owl:

- Developing another junior into a capable manager, or assisting with a significant project.
- Although recognition is not the objective for the owl, it is appreciated and it does help to continue the collaborative behavior.

Attributes often applied to the Owl:

- Wise
- Knowledgeable
- Dedicated
- Helpful
- Intelligent
- Logical
- Respected
- Sharp
- Confident
- Quiet
- Communal

Attributes not often applied to Owls:

- Lazy
- Extroverted
- Self-centered
- Ambitious
- Aggressive

P is for Piranha

Characteristics:

Piranhas are aggressive pack attackers, but are limited by their need to remain in water and their need for large numbers. Their feeding frenzies occur spontaneously when huge numbers of like-minded individuals attack as an uncoordinated thrashing group.

Piranhas don't flourish well on their own. They aggregate as equals in large groups without any overt organizational hierarchy. They are too restricted and protected by their need to exist in a special (water) environment. If they get into the wrong environment or are caught in receding waters they lose their advantage and are quickly overcome by other creatures. However, as a pack in their own territory, they are devastatingly dangerous and can rapidly overpower a beast many times their size and capability.

Relating to the Piranha:

A relationship with piranhas normally consists of eating them or being eaten by them. They have no reason for social graces or special preferences. They simply attack or avoid being attacked regardless of the creature that is in their territory.

There are some human instances where piranha-like frenzies can happen, but the human variety usually requires a ringleader to trigger the attack. Strikers can display the behaviors of the piranha. Some union movements and public political demonstrations can get out of hand when a charismatic leader instigates the masses to behave as an aggressive disorder that none of the individuals would do on their own.

In many organizations, gossipers can trigger emotional attacks or fan the fires of the rumor mill. Small clusters of like-minded individuals who stubbornly, even viciously, protect their own little territories for their own little reasons exist in many Zoos. Generally these packs are closely located, but they can go across multiple geographies in the modern world, where communications are no longer a barrier and traditional boundaries are not so restricted.

Piranhas see themselves as hungry and ready to attack anything that comes their way. Others see piranhas as dangerous if not controlled and best avoided.

Success for the Piranha:

- Taking down a larger beast to the benefit of the pack.
- The excitement of the feeding frenzy.

Attributes often applied to the Piranha:

- Swarming
- Aggressive
- Ravenous
- Dangerous
- Selfish
- Self-interested
- Frustrating

Attributes not often applied to Piranhas:

- Sincere
- Friendly
- Trustworthy
- Approachable
- Happy
- Individualistic
- Forward Thinking
- Trusting

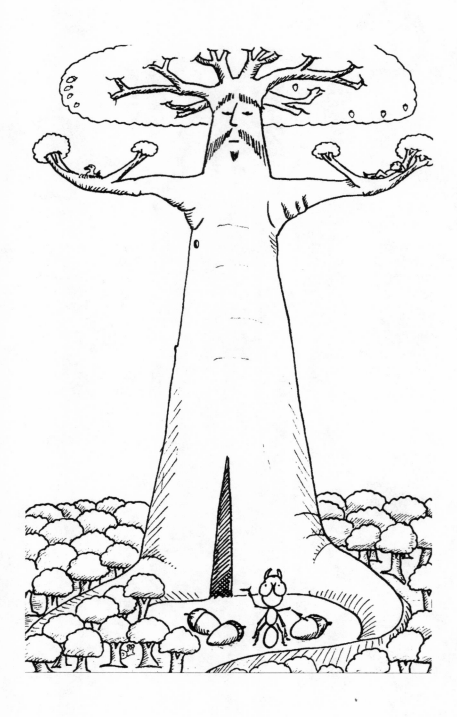

# Q is for *Quercus robur*

Characteristics:

Quercus robur is the scientific name for the common oak tree. The only plant in our Zoological Garden menagerie, it provides a necessary contrast for the creatures profiled here. All animals need to take energy from the environment, in the form of food, to survive. Ultimately they are dependent upon plants, so we must have at least one plant in the set of profiles to illustrate this role.

Most plants do not depend upon the creatures in their environment to survive, although they do have a relationship with many of them. Plants provide energy from outside the environment (through photosynthesis of sunlight), which is then used by the creatures, directly or indirectly. Plants also provide other forms of support for the animals like shelter and safety, for which they receive little or nothing in return. *Quercus* represents the best characteristics of plants. The oak is one of the most inspiring living creatures you will ever encounter. It is majestic and rugged, yet delicate and beautiful.

The oak does more than just provide nourishment and shelter. Its longevity and robustness serve as a source of inspiration to the community in which it lives. It generates oxygen to provide a breath of fresh air in the environment. It even buds both early and late in the season to ensure plenty of nourishment for all of the dependent creatures in the environment. Much of the energy created by *Quercus* benefits the wider community, in shelter and comfort for creatures from below the ground right up to the tips of the leaves.

People fitting this profile make a major contribution to organizations due to their selflessness, increasing the productivity of others and building confidence and morale. They help or mentor others simply for the enjoyment of it. Some *Quercus* people invest a great deal of their time performing charitable work, making a significant contribution of their own time and energy for no apparent return to themselves. Some non-executive board members play this role as much for the pleasure they experience when seeing their efforts generate benefits to the organization as for the pay.

Like *Quercus*, a great leader takes little from the immediate environment compared to what they give back. They provide support and fuel for the whole community around them. Great leaders generate energy from outside sources and pass this on to their own community in a selfless manner. Just as the creatures' survival depends either directly or indirectly on the oak, the culture, welfare and comfort levels of the people in a community are heavily reliant upon behavior and attitude of the community leadership.

Like the oak tree, *Quercus* people take a long time to mature and are often prematurely terminated before they develop to their full potential. In this disposable age, the attitude is often that everything must be done immediately, with the focus on extracting some quick benefits rather than maximizing long-term, sustainable benefits. A true *Quercus* cannot compete in such an environment and will therefore not be promoted or have influence on the decision makers. What they do provide is exploited and compromised for the short term, disappointing the *Quercus*.

Relating to *Quercus robur*:

If you are fortunate enough to have direct access to a genuine *Quercus*, you are privileged and will benefit from their inspiration. Unfortunately, very few get this opportunity as the real *Quercus* is rare. Where they do exist, it is often difficult to access them. However, you will gain from the enhanced environment that *Quercus* provides, through a mix of growth opportunities and shelter. The other creatures in your Zoo can support you better in an environment containing a *Quercus*.

If you get the chance to interact with a *Quercus*, have something engaging to say. Although they are generally busy, they do have time for others, especially those who show respect and intelligence. Triggering an intellectual exchange will get you noticed and perhaps could lead to better access. Perhaps even to a mentoring relationship! These are earned through demonstration of professionalism and respect for others. *Quercus* will only invest in those they consider worthy of assisting.

You do not need to have direct contact with *Quercus robur* to be positively influenced. Sometimes the mere sight of *Quercus robur*, or even a photo is sufficient to feel the inspiration and know the value that is provided by this unique entity.

Quercus see themselves as the historical balance in the Zoo and they know they need to inspire and support others. Most others show *Quercus* the appropriate respect and consider themselves honored to get some of their time. Some see *Quercus* as a threat, usually those with poor intent who know the *Quercus* will see through their thin disguises.

Success for *Quercus robur*:

- Positively influencing the members in the organization, especially the behaviors of the leadership team.
- They enjoy seeing others developing and prospering from their support and the application of their advice.

Attributes often applied to the *Quercus robur*:

- Inspiring
- Enthusiastic
- Knowledgeable
- Decisive
- Intelligent
- Parental
- Experienced
- Stimulating
- Reliable
- Philanthropic
- Approachable
- Rare

Attributes not often applied to *Quercus robur*:

- Selfish
- Disinterested
- Lazy
- Emotional

R  is for Rattlesnake

Characteristics:

Rattlesnakes are insecure politicians. They like to act aggressively and make a lot of noise when their plans don't go they way they want. If they find themselves in a position where they feel threatened, they take on what appears to be a highly attacking position, which is mainly defensive bluff. They may perform a threatening posture maneuver accompanied by copious noise. But if you observe closely, they usually hold their position or slowly back off while appearing in attack mode.

Rattlesnakes have specialized heat sensors so they can detect and track movements of other creatures in the dark. They use this capability to great advantage both for protection and for ambushing their prey (or enemies). They use their sharp forked tongue to sense chemical indicators in the air to read what is happening in the environment and also as a form of intimidation.

Relating to the Rattlesnake:

As long as you stay out of striking range of the rattlesnake, you are quite safe. They are normally all show and will not attack unless severely provoked or forced into a corner. But beware: If you push them too far, they are deadly when they get desperate. Under stress, they become vicious and go down fighting, taking as many enemies with them they can manage.

You need to be very careful when traversing unfamiliar environments, as you can unknowingly stress a rattlesnake simply by accidentally moving into their territory or even stepping on them if you don't hear their noisy complaints about your inappropriate actions. Remember, it is not your intention that matters. Simply your presence is enough to irritate the insecure rattlesnake and lead to a sudden, extremely accurate and dangerous counterattack.

The rattlesnake's heat sensors (corresponding to the rumor mill and eavesdropping) are constantly monitoring the Zoo's environment and their forked tongue can detect even the weakest political signals in the atmosphere. Some junior managers and some senior clerical staff may behave like a rattlesnake when stressed (perhaps mimicking their managers), but they simply don't have the potent venom to do much actual harm. Their rattles can be very loud if you get too close to their territory and it can be some fun to test your reflexes and hone your reactive skills against these less harmful varieties before taking on fully grown rattlesnakes in their own territory.

Rattlesnakes see themselves as the ones to highlight inadequacies and as protectors of their territory. They have confidence in themselves because they are capable of striking. However, others see them as the eternal bluffer and know to avoid them.

Success for the Rattlesnake:

- Scaring off the threat without needing to strike.
- Preventing the intruder from traversing their territory.

Attributes often applied to the Rattlesnake:

- Political
- Sharp
- Defensive
- Noisy
- Reactive
- Insecure
- Two-faced
- Divisive
- Survivor
- Adapted to harsh environments

Attributes not often applied to Rattlesnakes:

- Sincere
- Trustworthy
- Loyal
- Trusting
- Happy
- Pleasant
- Sociable
- Welcoming

S is for Sloth

Characteristics:

Sloths are an endangered species, mainly due to their slowness and inability to adapt to changing environments. Most Zoos, other than those dedicated to maintaining genetic diversity, do not bother to keep sloths as they are not exciting or particularly interesting to most people. This is an unfortunate situation as they have some unique abilities and a strangely intriguing set of habits that, if harnessed, could be of benefit, if only they remained awake for longer.

Sloths sleep between 15 and 18 hours a day, and most of their activities occur at night. They are mainly solitary creatures, having little interaction with other creatures or even their own kind. They do everything while hanging upside down in the treetops, including "walking" and sleeping, along with mating and giving birth. If forced to go to ground, they can walk upright, but they rarely do this and do not stay there for long before returning to their upside-down positions in the treetops.

These animals have specific adaptations to manage their bizarre slow, upside-down lifestyle, including cultivating algae in their coats, partially as camouflage and partially as a supplementary, easy to get at food source. Highly selective in what they eat, they are herbivores with limited range of fruits, leaves and flowers in their diet. As a result of their lifestyle, they are difficult for most prey to find and capture. One of their few natural predators is the eagle.

Relating to the Sloth:

If you have a sloth in your midst, you will have to maintain constant supervision and ensure that they remain active. Without this, they will simply doze off as they are just not made for the work force, especially daytime jobs. They are not inherently lazy, they just don't see the point of any unnecessary activities, which to them includes anything besides eating or sleeping, and maybe the occasional mating if the opportunity arose, but they do not go out of their way for it.

Sloths can be found in solitary-type roles, which do not require much activity or interactions with others. If they are forced to work interactively, they take every opportunity to slink off and find some spot to catch a quick undisturbed nap (lasting an entire morning or afternoon). Human sloths are found mainly on welfare and come to life on the Internet at about midnight, not for the social interaction, but just to occupy themselves until they can doze off again or potentially order in some food deliveries.

Sloths have no real friends or enemies. They don't consider how they see themselves and others don't usually see them enough to know what they are like.

Success for the Sloth:

- An unbroken siesta of about 12 hours, followed by another long nap not long afterwards.

Attributes often applied to the Sloth:

- Slow
- Weary
- Minimalist
- Submissive
- Lazy

Attributes not often applied to Sloths:

- Sociable
- Agile
- Enthusiastic
- Productive
- Busy
- Adaptable
- Communal
- Useful

T is for Triceratops

Characteristics:

These old battle-scared dinosaurs simply can't hack the pace any more. They have survived more changes to their environment than they ever asked for and wish the world would remain as it is now forever. This is not because they like it the way it is — in fact they are often miserable about the current state — but because they firmly believe more change will surely make the world even worse.

Their call-cry is "Been there, done that, didn't like it last time, either. Go away and leave me alone!" They have invested in maintaining the world the way it used to be. They use what power they have to fuel resistance, but normally it is not sufficient to prevent the inevitable changes.

Most triceratops have died out, but pockets of them are living on in hidden valleys in many organizations. In some Zoos, which the winds of change have bypassed, clusters of them survive even at senior levels.

Relating to the Triceratops:

To effectively relate to a triceratops, you must first convince them you are there to benefit them. This is not easy, as they have a great distrust of anyone they do not know personally and everyone who tries to sell them on an idea.

There is nothing a triceratops dislikes more than a young X-breed. In they come in with their advanced qualifications and a know-it-all attitude, attempting to push the triceratops around (or out of the Zoo completely). The battle between these two creatures can be extremely entertaining, if you ever get the opportunity to watch the joust without being noticed. The inexperienced youngster with only perceived clout attacks the immovable giant survivor from a past era. Neither have the required experience or tools to make much of a dent on the other without significant assistance from higher authority, and each is as stubborn as the other. With its massive armour shields, the triceratops can mount a very strong defensive hold for a long time. Although they are not fast, they are cunning and can land a very solid blow with their horns. Their sheer size can be a major barrier to shifting them from blocking the gateway to the future.

Take care to observe these conflicts from a reasonable distance and do not be seen chuckling to yourself, because if they see you enjoying your observations, they will turn on you and make you the target of their frustrations. Either combination can be a formidable enemy, and you don't want to fight both at once.

Triceratops see themselves as the only sane ones in the Zoo, believing everyone else is just following the latest fad change. Others see triceratops as negative blockers who resist moving into the present, let alone the future.

Success for the Triceratops:

- Avoiding or delaying change. Even more satisfying is seeing change programs fail.

Attributes often applied to the Triceratops:

- Weary
- Pessimistic
- Change-averse
- Xenophobic
- Battle-scarred
- Tough
- Negative
- Slow
- Reclusive
- Reflective
- Nostalgic
- Problematical

Attributes not often applied to Triceratops:

- Visionary
- Adaptable
- Astute
- Collaborative
- Open
- Opportunistic
- Youthful
- Social (except among other Triceratops)

U is for Unicorn

Characteristics:

Unicorns are the mythical creature of ultimate beauty. They possess many of the positive features of the rest of the creatures, but (apparently) none of the faults. They are beautiful, run like the wind, can fly, are powerful and are thought about in awe by other creatures. Nevertheless, they are either extinct or perhaps never existed.

If unicorns did exist, they would represent the perfect beast. Some creatures like to portray themselves as a unicorn, but they play the part only when it suits them. Those who genuinely believe they have evolved into a unicorn are of course suffering from self-denial or delusions of grandeur.

Relating to the Unicorn:

You don't need to relate to a unicorn, as you will never meet one, although you will no doubt meet many who claim to be one (pretender or deluded - you decide).

The closest you will ever get to a unicorn is if you are lucky enough to meet *Quercus robur,* but in reality, very few of us actually get that privilege, either. If you happened to get into the lift with a Unicorn or *Quercus*, remember that they don't have the time to hear your life story. You would want to leave them with a positive impression, so prepare.

Think about how to relate to those who believe they are unicorns. They are very interesting to study. Some genuinely cannot see their own faults (somewhat like some X Breeds) and truly believe they are the perfect being (bless their deluded souls). Others know they are living a lie, but like to generate the image of perfection in the eyes of those who cannot see the real truth. The attention and adoration they receive from their believers is the sustenance their ego thrives on. Pretend unicorns, however, prove unpredictable in crisis. They have a tendency to find fault in others when blame needs to be handed out. Self-blame is not an option, because they cannot admit that they made a mistake.

Paradoxically, a real unicorn would be able to see some shortfalls in their style, because to be perfect is to know that improvement is always possible. Most others can see right through the pretend unicorns, except for perhaps some dogs and kids. The kids learn with time, whereas dogs continue to have absolute faith in their unicorn masters.

Success for the Unicorn:

- For a real unicorn, success would simply be living. Everything they did would be perfect.
- For a pretend unicorn, success is being admired, seen as a success and remaining a legend through time.

Attributes often applied to the (pretend) Unicorn:

When they rate themselves:
- Perfect
- Visionary
- Open
- Honest
- Collaborative
- Everything positive

When rated by others:
- Arrogant
- Aloof
- Ambitious
- Controlling
- Dangerous
- Frustrating
- Insecure
- Inconsistent
- Nostalgic

Attributes not often applied to Unicorns:

When they rate themselves:

- Anything negative (except the implication that they don't exist, which comes from people with poor imaginations)

When rated by others:

- Realistic
- Self-conscious
- Open
- Stimulating
- Trustworthy
- Humble
- Honest
- Forward thinking
- Motivational

V is for Vulture

Characteristics:

Vultures prey on sick and wounded creatures in order to survive themselves. They lack the courage to attack healthy individuals for fear of them fighting back and causing them harm or injury. They gleefully scan the environment for others' misfortunes and patiently wait for the penultimate moment before death to pounce, because any further delay would lead to another vulture claiming the prize before they do. They squabble among themselves while waiting in anticipation and will vigorously compete over the pickings.

Relating to the Vulture:

Vultures can be trusted only to do one thing - to hover when you are most vulnerable. It does not matter who or where you are. If you look like being in a spot of bother, they will be hanging around to see if they can score an easy feed. This makes them no threat when you are in good condition and travelling well, but they are difficult to deal with when things are not so great. While they do not threaten others as such, their looming presence is distracting and can drag your spirits down. They degrade morale, and it is especially difficult for many to watch as they go about their work finishing off others less fortunate.

For the experienced Zoo observer, the circling of vultures unintentionally serves as a warning sign for trouble. Vultures have an extremely sensitive "nose." They can detect stressed individuals long before anyone else can and quickly start their gleeful circling of potential victims anticipating the inevitable. By watching vultures closely, you may be alerted to a problem that you can fix and ruin their fun.

Vultures are often frustrated middle to upper managers who have risen to (or beyond) their level of competence. Incapable of performing a clean "kill" of their own at this challenging level, they need to rely upon the easy prey to remain in existence.

Vultures see themselves as the pragmatists of the Zoo. They do the culling that others are not prepared to do by taking out the weakest members. Others see vultures as negative scavengers always ready to prey on those who are down on their luck.

Success for the Vulture:

- Watching a failure and then picking over the bones.
- Being negative about something before it happens and then being proven right (though they, or their negativity, may have also contributed to the demise of the subject).

Attributes often applied to the Vultures:

- Nasty
- Opportunistic
- Scavenging
- Self-centered
- Dangerous
- Political
- Competitive
- Sly
- Patient

Attributes not often applied to Vultures:

- Benevolent
- Trustworthy
- Happy
- Collaborative
- Brave
- Open
- Pleasant
- Social (even among their own)

W is for Whale

Characteristics:

Whales are magnificent creatures, a gigantic mammal surviving very well in an environment not designed for their kind, but to which they have become adapted. By becoming very specialized and highly knowledgeable about their environment, they can normally navigate large distances and repeatedly deliver their pods back through complex migration patterns year after year.

These highly social creatures travel in large pods and maintain long-term relationships within these social groups. They have highly sophisticated communication methods that can be well understood by other whales but not by any other type of creature.

The vulnerabilities of whales come from their strengths. The fact that they are highly specialized makes it difficult for them to cope with changes. They rely upon their vast knowledge and sophisticated social structures to lead them on their journeys. However, sometimes some whales make poor navigational decisions that can be fatal mistakes. If a bull-whale beaches himself, the rest of the pod will often simply follow him to their death. What is worse, if a whale is rescued, it often immediately turns round and makes the same mistake again.

Once they become disoriented, it is difficult for them to readjust. It is as if the information they have cannot be erased. Despite clear proof that they are doing something wrong, they continue their behavior, often to their final downfall.

Relating to the Whale:

Whales have much to offer through their vast knowledge and high intelligence, but communicating with them is extremely difficult as they have a completely different communication mechanism from others. They seem to know what other creatures are on about but don't see what it has to do with them. They politely and unobtrusively observe those trying to interact with them (probably for amusement as much as anything) and then continue on their path.

To get a whale's attention you must go into their environment and act as they do. If you are one of the lucky ones who get to interact with the whale, you may learn from this interaction. However, you can never learn more than a small fraction of what the whale knows. If you are even luckier again, you might know what to do with some of what you have learned, as for many of us the specialized knowledge they have is too abstract for us to apply.

Whales tend to aggregate in highly specialized roles such as technical specialists and information-rich or research-based professions. Such specialization makes it difficult to relate to them as they seem to be talking a completely different language.

In our results-driven environments, the whale is often overlooked and undervalued. In a constantly changing world, the information we have for decision making needs to be increasingly challenged to ensure validity and relevance. Often human whales are not good at this and find themselves beached as a result of blind belief that old-world rules still apply. As a result of these features, they are often seen as unreliable or an unnecessary luxury by those with small minds or a lack of imagination.

Because of their gentle nature and vulnerability, whale numbers have been greatly reduced by poachers who benefit from their demise. As we move into the age of retiring baby boomers and beyond, zookeepers will realize just how much value the whales have contributed and they will miss them severely.

Whales see themselves as highly sophisticated social beings capable of great journeys and amazing feats. Others see them as majestic, knowledgeable creatures that are difficult to understand and prone to occasional stupid acts.

Success for the Whale:

- Moving the pod through the next migration cycle.
- Gaining a new insight into a previously unknown problem.
- Mentoring the young whales and seeing them develop into fully capable whales in their own right.

Attributes often applied to the Whale:

- Intelligent
- Inspirational
- Knowledgeable
- Powerful

- Social
- Communal
- Self-limiting
- Accident-prone
- Reserved
- Gentle
- Endangered

Attributes not often applied to Whales:

- Adaptable
- Aggressive
- Lazy
- Arrogant
- Competitive
- Dangerous
- Manipulative

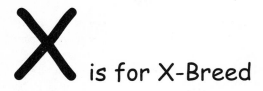 is for X-Breed

Characteristics:

X-breeds are multi-talented creatures specifically designed, bred and developed to perform. Through cross-breeding, they have acquired characteristics from several different creatures to create an artifical new thoroughbred super-species. They are designed to be hybrids, the best of the best and capable of anything.

However, as in the meaning of "X," X-breeds have an "unknown" in the equation. Hybridization techniques can generate a lot of undesirable combinations that are difficult to manage, cause internal conflicts or pose extreme dangers.

X-breeds can be created by traditional breeding techniques or through genetic manipulation. The liger (cross between a lion and a tiger) and the mule (combining donkey and horse) are good examples of the traditional approach. The range of Genetically Modified Organisms (GMO's) now appearing are the outcome of the latter. We are all a little cautious of GMOs, as they open a whole new range of opportunities but could also prove a real Pandora's box.

Zoos are the perfect place for cross-breeding, as they have so many different types of creatures at their disposal. You are bound to come across many X-breeds in your Zoo, especially in this era where career changes are very common. We get technical people trying to change their stripes to become managers, managers wanting to become mentors or CEO's and tradespeople becoming business owners. Sometimes the outcomes are fantastic and other times they are appalling. The old adage "jack of all trades and master of none" is a very common outcome of cross-breeding.

Imagine the futuristic Zoo where the zookeeper can be a "Dr. Moreau" capable of creating any set of characteristics he wants in his creature. If CEO's had this power, they would create a personal assistant with a cute face, beautiful aerodynamic form and positive demeanor, but what else? They could add the genes for well-camouflaged bone-crushing teeth with a schizophrenic "bite your head off" attitude – just in case you thought you might try to weasel your way into the big office.

Cross-breeding and genetic manipulation are not as simple as portrayed in the 1990's Hollywood film "Twins," where all of the positive features or all of the negatives appeared in one individual. As this science continues to advance, the scientists may get better at biasing the outcomes, but they are still a long way off being able to select characteristics from a menu to achieve desired outcomes. As any creature breeder will testify, selective breeding may deliver finer capabilities, but it often concentrates other problems. The overbred pedigree can show a variety of weaknesses not found in the common garden-variety mongrel, who is often more robust, resilient and stronger in the longer term.

Relating to the X-breed:

X-breeds can be difficult to work with, as each one is different and they can be somewhat schizophrenic. With an unnatural mix of characteristics from different species, you can never be sure exactly how they will react in different situations.

The objective, of course, is to deliver all of the positive characteristics from each of the source creatures. However, what is positive for the X-breed is not necessarily good for the other creatures that come into contact with them or in all situations.

While some X-breeds appear to be the perfect individual who has everything, they are blind to their own shortcomings. These over-achievers with inflated egos can be condescending and patronizing or even impatient. They do not understand why others struggle to perform what they consider basic tasks, like reciting the genetic code of the human being or calculating the rate of expansion of the universe from first principles. Accustomed to being the best at everything, X-breeds generally try to evade any opportunities for improvement or at least downplay them. Being supremely confident in themselves, they simply do not realize they have limitations or do not consider them important. They therefore can react negatively to offers of assistance to help them improve.

Some X-breeds have a natural capability to be good at everything, but these are rare. For most successful people their sheer natural ability, intelligence and "good breeding" has been supplemented with well-targeted development, insightful mentoring, good advice and a lot of hard work throughout their career.

Fast-track development is the traditional method for generating X-breeds, involving selecting the young talent and pushing them through a challenging program of cross-functional project involvement, international placement and mentoring programs. These young golden haired executives are normally targeted early (even during recruitment) as the successors of the business leadership. When well managed, such programs add great value to the business and the individuals alike.

However, in these times of short tenure, rapid change, constant restructures and low loyalties, such programs are less common, and successful ones even less common. The capabilities of the X-breeds arising from such programs are highly sought after, and many businesses find their young golden-haired execs lost to competitors before they receive benefits from their investments. This is almost inevitable, because cross-business experience is the only missing piece required to accelerate the rapid rise and satisfy the personal agenda of the X-breed. X-breeds are more ambitious than they are loyal and they don't trust a business to remain focused on the current succession plan, nor the assurances of the part they will play in it.

X-breeds are also generated through the ubiquitous MBA (Master of Business Administration) program. These courses are designed to provide everything the "New Manager" requires to bypass the corporate ladder and begin directly as a senior manager. Consultancy businesses and new business categories are full of bright young faces ready to "advise" highly experienced managers on how to run their business and to explain that what they are doing is wrong. They "know" this because they have learned it from the latest academic theories that have replaced all of the old-school thinking that simply is not applicable any more. Any teenager knows that "old stuff" is of no value at all and is happy to advise you to "Move on, as you are soooo last year."

The fresh faced MBA's and consultants justify all of this by telling you that the world is constantly changing, so you have to change what you do to keep up. No doubt, there are elements of truth to this. However, it is a severe mistake to drop everything you do now and replace it with all new stuff. Things that worked before will still have elements that can be adapted and remain highly valuable. New theories and practices will have some aspects that have not sufficiently evolved to be reliable in all circumstances. Who ever uses an alpha release of new software for critical functions? Well, maybe some dot-com failures did. The difficulties arise when those passionate about either the "new" or the "old" close their ears to the other side.

Although they just do not get along well together, old-style managers and the MBA's between them have a very powerful set of capabilities. The elders have the history, the learnings, the practical experience and the deep smarts, but sometimes lack awareness of new opportunities or the latest techniques. The MBA's have fresh knowledge and ideas but no experience. Review as many case studies as you like, it is still not experience. A returned assignment with some marks taken off is not the same as the burn of a poor business decision, scared into your memory with the knowledge that others know about your mistake.

MBA programs have generated some leaders who are admired and openly acknowledged as deserving to be where they are. However, deserved or not, success more often attracts gripes from others about how they unjustifiably obtained their role (or snide suggestions about who they know, or slept with, to get there).

The dot-com executive was a genetic transformation that combined the technology executive, the ultimate optimist and the "bovine-excrement artist" (smooth talk and little real business capability). These types were an experiment gone wrong as they were missing the "how to run a business based on fact and actually producing something of value" gene. The absence of this gene was not detected by unsuspecting investors (who mistakenly took the dot-com exec as the ultimate X-breed) until far too late. This shows the level of confidence people inherently have in the X-breed. Normally conservative, competent and sane managers dropped their guard and invested heavily without any facts to justify literally billions of dollars.

X-breeds see themselves as perfect unicorns or saviors of the Zoo. Most others see X-breeds as self-inflated and self-centered, but recognize their level of technical competence, even if some of the interpersonal aspects are a little lacking.

Success for the X-Breed:
- Creating wealth (mainly for themselves).
- Being seen with the "right people."

Attributes often applied to the X-Breed:
- Arrogant
- Verbose
- Selfish
- Ambitious
- Beautiful
- Busy
- Fashionable
- Extroverted

- Educated
- Capable

Attributes not often applied to X-Breeds:

- Thorough
- Experienced
- Trustworthy
- Tolerant
- Patient
- Adaptable (despite their design)
- Caring

Y is for Yak

Characteristics:

Yaks are lovable characters. You can't help but like them. They are amusing, non-political and larger than life creatures who enthusiastically contribute. They are always full of beans and looking to get on with the task at hand. The downside of the yak is their inability to plan well enough in advance and ensure that they have a balanced approach to what they are doing. They often trample the whole garden in order to water one thirsty plant. They are not deliberately destructive. They just get so excited and focused on what they are doing that they simply don't think beyond the immediate.

One yak friend of mine nearly flooded the cellar because by forgetting to turn off the water main before removing a tap to change a dripping washer. Another young IT graduate once deleted all of my computer files to resolve a minor file corruption problem. He happily gloated about fixing the issue quickly (which he did), but I could have lost days of work had I not backed up just before letting him at my machine. They are the type that can end up as Darwin Award nominees in extreme cases, or as victims in assault cases through lack of foresight. (The Darwin Award recognizes people who have died or seriously injured themselves while doing something extremely stupid.)

Relating to the Yak:

Yaks need close supervision and clear instructions, especially about potential risks. You need to talk them through each step and highlight what to look for to ensure that things are going to plan. If you are unfortunate enough to have a yak as a boss (deep sigh....I commiserate with you), you will have to learn how to upwardly manage in order to prevent disasters. Don't fear this too much, as yaks rarely rise too far up the Zoo hierarchy for obvious reasons.

Do not feed them after midnight, allow them near alcoholic beverages or dare them to do something stupid. You may be held accountable for their outcomes.

Yaks' friendly nature and can-do attitude make them quite well liked throughout the Zoo, until they make their inevitable clumsy mistake. Those burned by the experience will still like the yak, but be very careful before allowing them to charge into a project unsupervised.

On most teams, the yak makes a good team member. They see themselves as a "go-getter" who gets the job done (often completely oblivious to the collateral damage they cause). Others see the yak as a deliverer, but needing to be controlled. Generally others are comfortable dealing with yaks' laid back style.

Success for the Yak:

- Getting the current task done and having some fun along the way (hopefully without creating havoc, but they would not notice or plan for potential problems).

Attributes often applied to the Yak:

- Boisterous
- Happy
- Playful
- Energetic
- Enthusiastic
- Tactical
- Friendly
- Social
- Frustrating
- Serendipitous
- Focused (to the point of being unaware of potential collateral damage and risks)

Attributes not often applied to Yaks:

- Careful
- Patient
- Experienced
- Considerate
- Modest
- Meek
- Slow
- Strategic
- Self-aware
- Intelligent

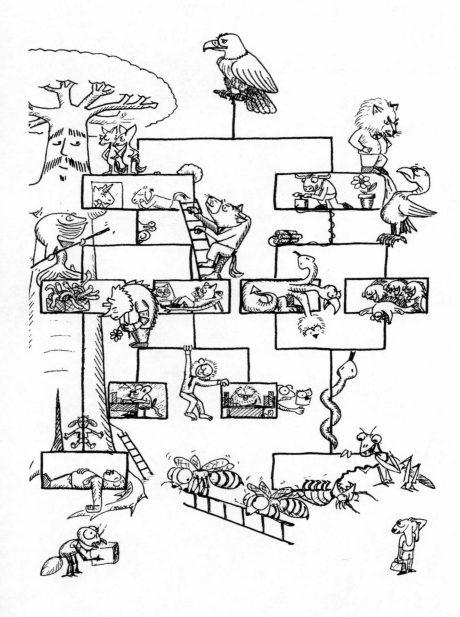

Z is for Zoo

Characteristics:

Each Zoo takes on a culture or a set of characteristics that depends upon the balance (or imbalance) of the creatures in the Zoo and the customer base that patronizes it. There are very aggressive Zoos and Zoos that are so passive they themselves become extinct, leaving their residents to either die with them, be set free, or transferred to another Zoo should they not be capable of surviving in the wild.

It is possible for creatures to live outside the Zoo, and indeed many of them take their chances at this and do very well. However, survival outside the Zoo as a free-ranging creature is a difficult challenge, as competing with the other free-ranging creatures takes more strategy and skill than being protected from them and having your food delivered daily inside the Zoo.

Surviving in your Zoo:

To survive in your Zoo, get to know all the other creatures and who their associates are as well as their enemies. Figure out why the friends are allies and why the combatants are enemies. Determine what you want from the organization and how you are most likely to get this without compromising your own values. Then align yourself with the appropriate people to achieve your goals. Make sure you closely monitor the activities of the enemy.

Many creatures in your Zoo will not want to let you know who they are or why they behave as they do. You should not inherently trust those who elect themselves as your guide dog and thrust themselves upon you to provide assistance. Always think about why they are doing that. They may be genuine like a gibbon or an owl, or they may have ulterior motives, like a vulture or lion (such as seeing you as tomorrow's breakfast). All Zoos are full of secret social networks, and unless you are part of them you don't even know they exist. Without being in these, you don't get the real lowdown, and you can't elect to join them. They are by invitation only, and the invitation comes only after a long assessment period of your behavior that you don't even know is happening.

To make your task even more difficult, those who look like they run the networks actually don't. Many who seem to be behaving as a network chief are either lapdogs of the real chief or are actually still on the outside, trying to get into the network. They are hoping to be noticed or assume the role by behaving as if they are already part of or leading the network.

Then, of course, there is a divergence between the outward image of the organization and the internal images. The outside images are to impress investors, financiers, governments and the public, to make them feel warm and fuzzy about the Zoo. As a new kid or an old dog moving to new turf, you have to read the website, the recent press articles and the sanitized public relations machine communications. However, it is equally important to find someone on the inside to get a real feel for the organization's values and policies on people development.

From my perspective (see the Glossary), you cannot know a Zoo's real values and policies without ever being inside it yourself, or having a close and trusted friend or family member in it who has seen both positive and negative situations managed. Alternative sources for your assessment are customers and suppliers of the Zoo you are interested in. You can't judge a book by its cover, but if you read enough reviews, you will at least be better prepared.

With careers, as with most activities in life, various recipes can increase your chances of a good outcome. However, there are never guarantees of success, despite many MBA schools assuring you their answer is the guarantee. Home-made recipes are generally better than packet-mix preparations, as you can then adjust any individual component to your own taste.

My own favorite recipe is this: First decide what it is you are creating. Then sample what is already out there and determine which suits you best or what new combination you wish to generate based on your flavor preferences. Collect your desired ingredients and do your homework by testing out some prototypes in your home kitchen to assess the quality of the outcomes. Perform your market niche assessment and add a dash of prevention before mixing. With a little planning, a pinch of realism and a heaped spoon of honesty, a tremendous amount of hard kneading to complement the appropriate rising time in the oven, you are bound to come out all right. Don't forget to preset the oven temperature and continue to monitor during cooking! And have a contingency plan in the freezer, just in case the home-cooked version does not turn out quite right. You'll have a temporary alternative without starving before you try your next (adjusted) batch. Remember that tastes change over time, including your own, so you may need a variety of recipes available to ensure a lifetime of successes.

Success for the Zoo

- Remaining in operation (preferably profitably), which requires adaptability, diversity and good management.

Attributes often applied to the good Zoo:

- Welcoming
- Friendly
- Diverse
- Open
- Inspiring
- Playful
- Pleasant
- Productive
- Respected
- Balanced
- Happy
- Social
- Stimulating
- Adaptable
- Trustworthy
- Caring
- Knowledgeable
- Interesting
- Confident
- Thinking
- Collaborative
- Visionary
- Worldly
- Extroverted
- Dedicated.
- Simply, THE place to be

Attributes often applied to the poor Zoo:

Antonyms of any of the above "Good Zoo" attributes list PLUS:

- Political
- Negative
- Vain
- Territorial
- Two-faced
- Backward
- Divisive
- Lazy
- Arrogant
- Frustrating
- Change-averse
- Selfish
- Insecure
- Manipulative
- Nasty
- Procrastinating
- Dangerous
- Endangered
- In summary, a place you should avoid

Part 2

Understanding the Zoo

The Character of the Zoo

The character of any Zoo depends largely on what its most influential creatures value. The senior creatures determine which creatures get access to which resources, who gets the biggest enclosures, best feed rations, most attention from the trainers and so on. Some senior creatures think big and must have major displays from all round the world while other creatures prefer their own little personalized, private Zoo for their own purposes and pleasure. Think of the Melbourne (Australia) or San Diego (United States) Zoos versus a suburban backyard with a fish-pond and an aviary. There are some people who want to spend time in a backyard and look at the five fish and three birds. Others expect nothing short of a wild safari traversing many continents.

The attitude of the dominant creatures defines the level of interest external creatures have in getting into your Zoo. Some creatures desperately seek a big Zoo in which to flourish, whereas others would die in a big Zoo. The trick to leading a happy career is to find a Zoo that suits your style and that is dominated by the type of creature you want to be.

Some small organizations add tremendous wealth to the world, in cultural areas (Museum of Modern Art), health areas (the Dr. Fred Hollows Foundation) or through community support activities (charities). There are Zoos that transform themselves in size, vision or culture to a whole new paradigm. Microsoft Corporation went from a small one-man operation to one of the biggest Zoos in the world. Enron and WorldCom made the opposite transformations. Why does that happen? Which path is your Zoo on? What role will you have in this change?

So Why Am I in the Zoo Anyway?

Zoos are essential for many creatures, some because they depend completely upon the Zoo for food and shelter and others because there is no longer a natural habitat sufficient for them to live in. Still others are not invited into the Zoo, but choose to live there because it is an easy life for them. For example, some birds and rodents are attracted into the Zoo, despite it not being their natural habitat. They come because there is plenty of left-over food and lots of shelter, even protection from potential predators. They can live there very well, compared to the difficulties of making the most of natural environments.

In the Zoo, many creatures are forced to live in close proximity to others they could not survive with naturally. All sorts of artificial barriers are put in place with the need for hunting removed. This places great stresses on the creatures, because despite the barriers and the free provision of foods, they are what they are and their natural behaviors no longer apply. They cannot simply ignore (depending upon your belief) a couple of million years of evolution, the creator's pre-coded instructions, or their destiny. They have to behave according to their instincts. The grassland dwellers should immediately go into flight at the sound of a lion's roar or the smell of a hyena, but this simply is not appropriate in a Zoo.

In a Zoo, predators can enter your cubicle and taunt you simply by their presence, and you have to live with these stresses. Like Zoos, organizations are very unnatural places in which many inhabitants would not choose to be, if they had other options available and were not tied there somehow.

Some human creatures do choose to escape from the Zoo and take their chances at the more risky, but more satisfying free-range lifestyle.

Freed creatures find a niche for themselves that supplies adequate food and shelter for their clan. Some prosper greatly from this, while others struggle, yet are happier outside the Zoo. Others who have been in captivity for too long either perish outside or give up and return to the Zoo to make the best they can of an environment they are not happy with, but which offers more stability and food. However, in doing so, they compromise their freedom.

Is There a Typical Zoo?

There is a complete range of Zoos out there—everything from small to large, selfish to philanthropic, private to public, honest to, well, interpreting the rules with a different perspective. There are "fly by night" and backyard operations, which appeared last week, but were gone yesterday, right through to socially active, global organizations that have been around almost since two cavemen traded spears and everything in between. Unfortunately, the two cavemen neither thought to register their intellectual property or their hunting territories, and men have been fighting about who owns what ever since. This eventually resulted in rules of engagement, leading to lawyers and governments and soon enough, legal battles and wars. Not all development is necessarily good.

How do you know which type of Zoo to associate yourself with? You need to find one that has similar values and ethics to yours and that has the innovation and customer base to support a long and enjoyable career for you. Yes, I know, a tall order—but it will not happen if you don't at least try to meet your specifications. This may be the main reason why the average executive has five major changes in their career path, although a constantly changing world also has a significant effect on this.

Survival Techniques

We humans have a lot we can learn from our creature friends about how to survive and adapt to changing conditions. Creatures have adopted a wide range of techniques over the millennia, some of which are simple for humans to adopt and can provide great success. Some are more effective than others, depending upon your situation and who else is in your Zoo.

For many creatures, mere survival is the aim of the game. To think beyond today's existence is a luxury they cannot afford. Such creatures are highly tactical in their behaviors and are generally reacting to their environment. Survival techniques for them include these:

Aggression	Attacking others either to overpower them or prevent being overpowered by them first. This is often accompanied by the element of surprise to increase advantage. Crocodiles have been masters at this since before humans appeared on earth.
Leadership (lion style)	Physical strength and fear succeed for a while, but eventually another creature comes along who is younger, stronger and with the attitude to defeat the leader. Those who lead by fear eventually die by their own mechanisms.
Hiding and/or camouflage	Being invisible does not guarantee survival, but it helps. Many creatures employ this strategy, but for some humans being invisible is simply not acceptable as they need to be discovered and heavily rewarded to feel happy.
Assertiveness	Defensively holding their own territory without outwardly attacking others. Wombats have a hard bone in their rump for when a predator follows them into their burrow. They suddenly thrust upwards crushing the head of their assailant against the burrow roof. Fighting on your terms and on your own territory has a lot going for it.

Ubiquity	The individual survives simply by being one of a large number spread everywhere. This is of course a numbers game and you could still be the next fish in the school to be taken by the shark.
Dependencies	Dependent relationships afford some protection and shelter to many simple creatures. These can be symbiotic (mutually beneficial) or parasitic, when one benefits at the expense of the other. Both forms of these relationships occur with plants and creatures and are clearly evident in many human organizations.
Endurance	The ability to keep your head low and your morale high when things are not to you liking. Sometimes you can endure the (often short) time until the next restructuring, when things have changed (we hope for the better). With a little luck the lion you have now will be replaced by an eagle, and the whole situation will become a positive again. Don't hold your breath, though, as such changes are slow and take a lot of effort to be successful. They also have enemies who resist the changes or actively undermine them.
Accountability	Being completely and utterly responsible for one's own actions. You don't often see any creatures (other than humans) taking life-threatening risks. There is a good reason for this, of course (and we think that we are the smart ones!). Remember too that we are the only creature who has a legal system that can transfer responsibility to someone else regardless of how stupid we have been.

Flourishing Techniques

Life is not always tough for everyone. Some of us have the ability and foresight to look beyond the immediate term to prepare for what might eventuate (usually a luxury restricted to those in positive Zoos). Even better, some of us can predict what might happen and build contingencies. Or better again, we can imagine what we want to happen and manipulate the circumstances to our advantage so as to maximize the chances of achieving the optimal outcome. Whoever is in the last category is flourishing rather than surviving. Flourishing techniques that can be adopted are summarized in the following table.

Leadership (eagle style)	Migrating birds have the inner strength and confidence to complete Herculean tasks through mental strength and inspiration. The vision and knowledge required to undertake such major changes on a regular basis are something to hold in awe.
Motivation	The wild stallion inspires herd members with alertness, quick thinking, bold actions and physical strength. Being positive and confident are a big part of the inspiration. Creatures follow bold actions, not idle chatter.
Maturity	Creatures ignore activities of others that are trivial or those that have no direct impact upon them. Humans have not learned this valuable behavior. We make the mistake of getting involved in all sorts of things that really don't matter, especially when they are other people's business. This is very time consuming and often a waste of time at best, and harmful to you or others at worst. Maturity provides you with the ability to determine what really matters.
Productivity	By producing more than you need, you can get through the tough times and even create some excess for sharing with others, like *Quercus robur.*
Pro-activity	Don't wait for fate to happen to you. Drive your own destiny by being ahead of the pack like the early bird.
Collaboration	The outcome of a collective effort is always better than that of a single individual if collaborative processes are right. Don't waste the opportunity to benefit from another or to help another where you can.
Networking	You are as capable as your entire group of associates, if you treat them well. Networking is an evolutionary advance from dependency. Networking builds reliable bridges and trust among members.

Control	Observe your environment and take control of what is happening. You do not have to control the whole environment, just the areas that can lead to maximizing benefits to yourself or your part of the Zoo. Control is critical to maintain a stable foundation, but should not be so rigid as to prevent improvement or innovation.
Awareness	Remain aware of what is going on both within and outside of your immediate environment. Maintain active networks and a vigilant watch to monitor activities and trends. Meercats do this very effectively. They rotate the watch shift and quickly communicate dangers to the entire group. Watching can be for potential opportunities as well as threats.

Communities, a Very Different Type of Zoo

Despite slow improvement in the face and nature of Zoos, there is a growing shift of some creatures away from the traditional Zoo. These tend to be the more knowledge focused creatures as they obtain more professional and personal rewards from mixing with their own types in a less formal community. Such communities are generally dependent upon voluntary participation and involved parties are not paid for their contributions. So what drives these creatures to participate in an activity among others whom they may never meet (if the community is virtual)? Why are they prepared to shun their own Zoo and pass on their knowledge to strangers for no reward? This does not seem to be a logical evolutionary process or even a good strategy for survival in the short term.

This learned behavior has more to do with the stress of living in the artificial environment of the zoo than anything else. In the Zoo, members are treated as objects of observation and entertainment. They must perform in a way that attracts the crowds and that therefore creates value for the Zoo, or they will be replaced by another creature. Some creatures flourish in this setting; they love the attention and the stresses (sold as "challenges" by the Zoo), and they do very well both personally and financially.

Others do not lust for the public attention but still want quiet recognition for the value they provide. When recognition does not come (often because their value is claimed by others feeding from their knowledge and selling it as their own), they become disheartened or demoralized.

They start to seek the recognition elsewhere by helping others who need it. They prefer to assist those who genuinely appreciate it, than serve those who demand and quickly denigrate them if work is not completed.

These voluntary communities are Zoos, but very different ones from those we have discussed in the rest of this book. They exist as a wide range of loose types: the mothers' group, the social club, the church community, the online virtual specialist or knowledge management group. The community is all about trust, recognition and mutual benefit. The benefits are not financial, but involve knowing that a positive contribution is being made and that beneficiaries do appreciate the efforts. This is usually reward enough for the volunteers, but they hope that the beneficiaries will "pass it on" and bring benefits to others as well.

Community participants genuinely like helping others. They like the lively interchange of ideas, the open conversations, the constructive criticism and the fact that community debated subjects always get a better outcome than most individuals bring about by working alone.

The community is more of a well-balanced environment, maybe more like an open plains Zoo, but with no boundaries at all. Creatures can come and graze as they desire and interact as they please. They can come as often as they like and leave whenever they want, most unlike the corporate Zoo. Community Zoos satisfy the mind and spirit, but unfortunately for most westernized humans, corporate Zoos are still necessary to fulfill the practical aspects of life like food and shelter.

The community Zoo is where most of us would be found if we existed only in spirit and did not have to worry about the practicality of providing food and shelter for ourselves and our families.

The Zoological Organization Chart

While a Zoo lacks the natural food-chain hierarchy that exists in the wild, it certainly does require a particular balanced hierarchy in order for the Zoo to function efficiently. As George Orwell put it, "We are all equal, but some are more equal than others."

Figure A shows a very well-balanced Zoo with a well-established food chain and the correct creatures with the right characteristics in the right places. By contrast, Figure B shows a very poorly balanced Zoo, one which would be very difficult to survive in. If there was ever any external pressure, this Zoo would become extinct.

Ideal Zoos:

The ideal Zoo has a very balanced mix of positive creatures. They have good diversity and collaborate freely through sharing knowledge and experience. The younger members of the Zoo are positively influenced by the leaders, who are individually, as well as collectively, inspirational and forward thinking.

Each member of the upper echelon of the organization voluntarily takes a direct interest in the development of some of the younger members and mentors them to become more capable and valuable members of the organization. The yaks learn to be more careful and considerate in their actions, the bees get significant and challenging tasks in early development stages, the dogs are trained well. Whales make positive contributions by being part of many project teams. The diverse mix in the cross-functional teams in ideal Zoos generates highly innovative ideas and creative approaches for implementing them. Team mem-

Figure A. The Well-balanced Zoo

Level in Zoo	Business equivalent	Mix of creatures often found
Patron	Chairman	*Quercus robur*
Zookeeper	Chief Executive Officer	Eagle (supported by Jackals)
Facilities managers	Senior management	Owls, Whales, Lion (supported by Jackals)
Specialists and creature handlers	Middle management	Owls (to be), Bees, Dogs (experienced), Yak (in training) (supported by some experienced Mice)
Support staff	Support staff	Mice, Bees (recent graduates/ interns), Kids, Yaks, Young Dogs and lots of Ants

bers inspire each other and value the insights and positive outcomes provided by the different perspectives other members have.

Ideal Zoos have little need for insects, as their whales, owls and bees in particular are very aware of the external environment. They are constantly searching new fields for resources and new opportunities to prosper from. They have a creative team feeding off this newly shared information and generating some completely new opportunities. Some of these ideas are so impractical that they are not viable, albeit interesting concepts. However, some can be adapted to become truly ground-breaking new opportunities. With some shaping work from the more action-oriented practitioners in the organization these opportunities become the next winners for the Zoo.

Creatures in this Zoo look up to the higher levels to determine how they should act, to learn values and to seek help.

Figure B. The Imbalanced Zoo

Level in Zoo	Business equivalent	Mix of creatures
Patron	Chairman	Lion, X-Breed, Triceratops
Zookeeper	Chief Executive Officer	Lion, Vulture or former Insect (supported by overzealous Jackal)
Facilities managers	Senior management	Rattlesnakes, Hyenas, Feline, Triceratops, Vultures (supported by politically motivated Jackals)
Specialists and creature handlers	Middle management	Yaks, Chameleons, Sloths, Felines, misguided Dogs (supported by Snails or Kids)
Support staff	Support staff	Kids, Yaks, Young Dogs and Nematodes

Zoos to avoid:

Negative Zoos can continue to exist if they are in the right type of external environment and don't have effective competitors. However, what happens to most is that they are so internally focused that the positive creatures migrate and start a new Zoo with a positive culture that ultimately out-competes the original one.

Such Zoos are negative as a result of an overabundance of the wrong creatures, especially in higher or more influential positions. The upper echelons have more interest in competing with their peers than in competing with other Zoos. They lose sight of the desired output of the Zoo and what the Zoo needs to do to prosper in the longer term. They make short-term tactical decisions that they personally benefit from rather than decisions that are for the good for the future of the zoo.

The creatures further down the food chain in this Zoo fear the upper levels. This fear creates apparent order, yet chaos reigns behind the scenes. The lower levels are simply resources consumed by those at the top.

Creatures in this Zoo look up to the higher levels to know when to hide.

Your Zoo:

Most Zoos are neither as good nor as bad as the extremes portrayed above. However, with a little analysis you can construct a picture of your Zoo, starting with your organizational hierarchy and filling in the boxes with creatures. It will soon become apparent whether you have a balanced ecosystem that will survive in the longer term or a challenged Zoo that is going backwards.

Most Zoos are somewhat schizophrenic in that they have teams that are very positive in among others that are extremely negative, inwardly competitive or aggressive. A good way to measure your Zoo is to look at the turnaround of the young people. There is no use citing a significant percentage of long-serving staff, if all of these are at the top.

Success comes from delivering a steady stream of kids and pups and investing in their development. This investment delivers dividends when some of these home-developed kids and pups develop into strong senior managers and leaders. If you don't convert enough of the kids and pups, you are not providing the right environment and not actively mentoring. You will always need to recruit externally, which costs Zoos heavily, both through lack of loyalty and loss of knowledge.

Part 3

Additional Resources

This section describes a number of ways in which the concepts in this book may be used for professional development and to drive cultural change. The tools are deliberately simple and most are designed to be performed in short exercises as part of other programs.

The following workshop games don't require any special tools or preparation, as they are meant to be performed quickly to enable learning in a fun atmosphere.

Creature Introductions

Attribute Ice Breaker

Network Diversity Analysis

Business Partner (or Competitor) Analysis

Glossary

Creature Introductions

Creature Introductions is a great way for some of our Zoo residents to understand each other in a fun way to trigger better interactions. It is a great ice-breaker at training events, inductions or workshops. Describing yourself or your environment with a creature metaphor depersonalizes the description and makes it a safe discussion topic. The differences that people come up with are often very surprising and usually lead to lot of fun for all.

Ask each of the participants at the event to describe themselves as a particular creature that they believe reflects their character. These creatures can be real, hybrids, mythical or genetically manipulated. The key is to get them to describe the characteristics that most reflect their behaviors and how they react to provide some insights to their personality and open up conversations in a fun way.

In an interesting alternative version of this game, have participants describe the whole organization as a creature or an ecosystem. Is the food chain balanced or not? How robust is it? Would it resist major environmental changes? Does it need some?

Sample outputs for the Creature Introductions game:

What creature are you?	**I am an ant.**
What characteristics does this creature have that relate to you (positive or negative)?	I like to work hard and enjoy being part of the team. I love the social structure in my work environment and I know that I can depend upon my friends as much as they can depend on me. I like what I do even though I am virtually invisible to the higher levels of management and (from their perspective) non-distinguishable from the other ants in the colony.
What creature are you?	**I am a lion.**
What characteristics does this creature have that relate to you (positive or negative)?	I am the leader in this jungle and I rule this territory over all other beasts. If you enter my territory, you get what you deserve, namely, to be captured by the members of my pride (who all hunt on my behalf) and be eaten.

Describe your organization as a creature.	**My organization is a mouse.**
Describe why you chose this creature.	It is small, but very agile and quick to take advantage of any crumbs that appear in its territory. It cannot compete with the many other larger creatures that it cohabits with. However, it survives well as it keeps a lower profile. Its flexibility and mobility keep it in the main game as an auxiliary player. I feel comfortable here as it is really alive, surviving on both mental and physical agility. Every day is unpredictable, but is a rewarding challenge and we live at a great pace.
Describe your organization as a zoo or ecosystem.	**My zoo is an open plains large cat sanctuary.**
Explain the reasoning behind this choice.	It is difficult to survive in the aggressive, competitive environment as the dominant residents are very aggressive and dangerous. This Zoo is very much an unnatural environment. It is not well balanced, being focused on only one type of creature and highly dependent on external intervention. If circumstances altered, the creatures and the whole environment would perish. Everyone feels this dependency and pines for the open plains, where they could hunt for real rather than have food drops. However, they don't realize this is not a real option as they would not survive outside this protected environment. Everyone is frustrated, and no one is really happy, and this results in internal bickering among the major players. Boredom is a common chronic condition.

Attribute Ice Breaker

There are over 150 attributes used in the creature profiles, sometimes in a negative sense and sometimes in a positive sense. A small set of attributes can be very effectively used to provide a good character profile of people or organizations without being too threatening. In your next meeting where people don't know each other, give them the list of attritutes on the following page and ask them to list the five words that most apply to them and another five that least apply to them. This can be a lot of fun, and if done with a modicum of honesty can provide some useful insights to get the relationships started and some networking happening.

A variation of this is to use the attributes to have everyone describe the creature they want to be and compare this to how they would currently describe themselves. The difference becomes their development target. You can then determine what your strategy will be to get more of the characteristics required to be what you want to be and fewer of your current characteristics that are inconsistent with your desired state. Don't be discouraged by the old adages "A leopard can't change its spots" or "You can't teach an old dog new tricks." They may not be able to, but you can if you really want it badly enough.

However, don't forget that a profile is only as accurate as the assessment. Self-assessment can be a little subjective, and it is always advisable to get a few other people's perspectives to be sure you are being realistic about your true profile. Often people answer with how they want to be rather than how they really are.

Attributes

Accident-prone	Divisive	Mature	Sensitive
Accountable	Economical	Modest	Serious
Action-oriented	Emotional	Motivated	Shy
Adaptable	Endangered	Motivational	Sincere
Aggressive	Energetic	Naive	Slow
Agile	Enthusiastic	Nasty	Sly
Ambitious	Experienced	Negative	Social
Approachable	Extroverted	Noisy	Sophisticated
Arrogant	Fashionable	Nostalgic	Stimulating
Assertive	Flexible	Open	Strategic
Astute	Focused	Opportunistic	Streetwise
Awesome	Forward-thinking	Organized	Strong
Backward	Frank	Parasitic	Submissive
Balanced	Friendly	Parental	Survivor
Battle-scarred	Fruitful	Patient	Swarming
Beautiful	Frustrating	Pessimistic	Tactical
Benevolent	Fun-loving	Pestiferous	Territorial
Boisterous	Gentle	Philanthropic	Thinking
Brave	Gullible	Playful	Thorough
Busy	Happy	Pleasant	Tolerant
Careful	Hardworking	Political	Tough
Caring	Holistic	Positive	Trusting
Challenging	Honest	Powerful	Trustworthy
Change averse	Humble	Present-focused	Two-faced
Collaborative	Inclusive	Problematic	Ubiquitous
Communal	Individualistic	Procrastinating	Vain
Communicative	Insecure	Productive	Verbose
Confident	Inspiring	Quiet	Visionary
Considerate	Instinctive	Rare	Weak
Consistent	Intuitive	Reclusive	Weary
Controlling	Intelligent	Reflective	Welcoming
Cool	Interesting	Reliable	Wise
Cunning	Invisible	Reserved	Worldly
Dangerous	Jealous	Respected	Xenophobic
Decisive	Knowledgeable	Scheming	Youthful
Dedicated	Logical	Self-aware	Zealous
Defensive	Loyal	Self-interested	
Diverse	Manipulative	Selfish	

Network Diversity Analysis

Natural ecosystems flourish when they have diversity and become polluted or unsustainable when there is an imbalance. The diversity provides balance with a niche for each type of creature. The balanced food chain ensures that no one type of creature becomes completely dominant.

In human Zoos, people often build their network only or primarily among people they feel comfortable with. This creates an imbalance, without enough diversity to challenge the environment, which becomes stagnated. The best ideas, innovations and solutions come from diversity and adversity. Rather than soliciting support from those who think like you, it is better to throw the idea out there to be attacked by those who think differently. This is necessary to confirm the robustness of the idea and to find ways to improve it. People who think like you see the same opportunities and problems that you do and miss the same risks. But people who do not think like you see other options and other issues you have missed. Yet it is harder to build trust and a workable relationship with those who do not think like you, as this invariably involves disagreeing with each other. Although this difference creates the strength in the relationship, it also usually leads to relationship failures, as emotions and egos get in the way of constructive dialogue.

Diversity of thinking and emotional reactions are necessary to provide thorough challenges and opportunity assessments for ideas and problems. "Left field" solutions usually appear to happen accidentally, but they shouldn't. They happen because someone took a totally different perspective on the situation and found a completely different way forward (sometimes successful and other times not so successful).

Try the exercise on the following page to highlight how to make diversity work for you.

Exercise: Building a diverse network

1. Take a blank sheet of paper and draw a circle representing yourself in the middle.

2. Closely around your circle, draw one circle for each person you frequently interact with (daily, weekly or every few weeks) for advice. Add their name to the circle.

3. More widely around your "inner circle," draw another set of circles representing those you interact with infrequently (monthly or less often).

4. Draw some connections representing relationships between these people: bold lines for the strong or frequent interactions and dotted lines for infrequent or casual relationships.

5. On the back of the sheet, make a list of those whom you rarely solicit feedback from or interact with, but who are related to your objectives. For instance, they work for the same organization or have a vested interest in your organization.

6. Review your diagram and confirm its completeness.

7. Now write on each circle which Zoo profile each of these people have.

NOTE: Try not to be too analytical about these diagrams your first time through. Go with your initial feel. You can adjust later if appropriate.

Analysis

- Are they all the same types or similar?

- Do you have some relationships that offer a completely different perspective from your own or from those similar to you?

- How can you build more diversity into your network?

- Can you create some relationships with some people from the back of your network analysis sheet?

- What benefit is there in establishing relationships with people from a totally different perspective from you?

Business Partner (or Competitor) Analysis

You can use the Zoo character profiles to determine the behavioral patterns of your business partners so that you can build better relationships with them. The better you understand your customers, vendors, allies and competitors, the more productive are your relationships (or competition) with them.

Thinking objectively about how they behave, what they like and dislike enables you to be proactive about how you interact with them. List the salient properties of their behavior and their strengths and weaknesses. Where can your strengths complement theirs and vice versa? How are they going to want to "play the game"? How will you win their attention, respect and loyalty? For competitors, the same principles apply, except you are trying to exploit their weaknesses and reinforce your vulnerabilities to withstand their attacks.

For example, would a lion customer be more impressed with tickets to the ballet, the football or a boxing match? What about that whale in your subcontracted research program? Do you offer the whale the same incentives as to the lion? Do you provide that outdoor hunting jacket or send them a subscription to the Discovery Channel?

Regardless of what you are, you need to build a workable relationship with those who are important to your success. This requires finding synergies between you and them. How does a mouse build a relationship with a lion? How does an owl optimize necessary interactions with a rattlesnake?

Building positive business partner relationships is a three-step process:

1. Correct diagnosis of the profile of your business partner.

- Are they stable and consistent?

- What influences their perspectives?

- What motivations and objectives do they have?

- Are these aligned with yours?

- How do you address fundamental differences?

2. Correct diagnosis of your own behavioral patterns and how you are perceived by the creature you need to interact with.

- How objective can you be about your own behavior?

- Are you able to get some honest objective feedback from someone you trust? Take care that you don't just hear what you want to hear, or get told what someone thinks they should say.

- Do you know how to interact with them?

- Do you really understand what they think of you?

- Are you perceived to be a potential predator, a competitor or are you just prey?

3. Careful planning of where the synergies are and what you can leverage to build on these synergies.

Glossary

Here you'll find definitions of words that apply to the Organizational Zoo. The definitions may differ slightly from how you might use the word in a general sense. As you probably know, many Zoos have their own language and specific jargon that you have to get to know in order to feel part of the team. Sometimes this language is more acronyms than actual words, especially if swarms of insects are about.

Jargon is deliberately used by the more political members of the Zoo as a means of showing themselves to be more in the know. They take great delight in being asked what a certain "TLA" (Three Letter Acronym) means as this demonstrates to all sufficiently privileged to be in their presence how knowledgeable they are. It also publicly reinforces their own perception of themselves as superior beings. A fun thing to do is to make up a TLA and use it on them and watch as they try to figure it out without the indignity of having to ask you what it means (which they will never do in public). Make sure you have an answer just in case they call your bluff.

Behavior

Scientists have studied creature behaviors for hundreds of years, and yet we still cannot predict the outcomes of many simple situations, let alone complex ones. We have managed to find ways to slowly modify behaviors of individuals, but we struggle to modify the behavior of groups. Since behaviors are inbuilt for many individuals and reinforced by cultural expectations, reprogramming them is difficult. When you consider the challenge of behavior modification for an individual, then you begin to understand the extreme difficulty of changing the behaviors and culture of an organization.

Botanical

All of the great Zoos around the world have a wonderful botanical setting in which the creatures can feel comfortable and safe. The more this botanical environment looks, feels and smells like the natural environment of the creatures, the better the health of the creature and the character of the Zoo overall.

Business organizations are no different. While the work comes from their creatures, their botanicals greatly contribute to the physical environment built around the workers so that they feel comfortable, safe and valued. After all, when you first visit a workplace, you get a feel for the company even before you speak to anyone. You develop a sense of the overall character of the company based on both the environment and individual attitudes amidst the overall culture of the organization.

Chemistry

There is a natural chemistry in all relationships. In humans, we see it in how well people naturally form partnerships or in explosions that occur when they come into close proximity.

Culture

Culture has several dictionary definitions, but the one I like most is "The sum total of the attainments and learned behavior patterns of any specific period, race or people" (or creatures). Another useful definition is "the development and refinement of mind, morals or taste." These two in combination serve the well-balanced organizational Zoo very well. They collectively cover what culture is, as well as an action that can be performed in order to improve the culture.

The characteristics of individuals within a culture vary, but if they stray too widely, cultural pressures will check their behavior or, if they are too extreme, bring about their excommunication from the culture.

Consider this in the context of the culture of your Zoo. If you do not like the culture, you have several choices; live with it (and experience the built-up anxiety that goes with this), bitch about it (which makes no difference, except that you feel better), change it (if you have the strength and capability to achieve this), leave it (move on to another Zoo where you like the culture) or form your own new Zoo with a culture more to your liking. These options are not mutually exclusive. In fact, common combinations include living with it and bitching about it or bitching about it and attempting to change it in small ways over time.

Changing the culture in a big way is beyond the capability of most Zoo residents, which is why partnering is so important. Groups of creatures with a vision and clear goals can effect cultural change, provided they have strong leadership and good teamwork. The team requires a diversity of skills, and if they are well intentioned and patient, they will normally achieve the desired changes.

Development

Development consists of making incremental improvements in the characteristics and behaviors of the creatures. This may involve the addition of characteristics not previously present but more often involves the enhancement of a characteristic already present.

A comprehensive development program has a wide scope of education to enable understanding of vital relationships between cause and effects. In addition, it targets enhancement of capabilities such as cognitive skills, strategy development, lateral thinking, complexity theory, sense making, people capabilities, communication skills and problem solving. Only through mastering these capabilities do leaders develop.

Teaching a dog to fetch a stick may be fun, but it is not development. The dog does not achieve much from those other than exercise and entertainment. However developing a dog's senses and educating it to identify and locate hidden drugs illustrates what an advanced development program can accomplish. Afterwards, the creature is not just faster, stronger or more efficient, it is almost a new creature, with finely tuned new capabilities.

Evolution

Evolution is the process whereby the characteristics of creatures and composition of the food chain are altered, leading to a new balance and a different set of behaviors in the environment. Evolution can result from a gradual series of minor adaptations to improve performance in a reasonably constant environment. It can also happen quickly as a result of a sudden major change in the environment. For example, the quality movement in the 80's made some significant improvements in performance before it faded. These improvements have become part of the new expected behaviors for Zoos rather than being lost. This resembles bacteria becoming resistant to antibiotics. They are more formidable after the change and can continue to become more resistant with more time. Global restructuring is an example of sudden evolution, which instantly changes the fortunes of most creatures and after which the whole ecosystem balance will never be the same. This resembles when the meteorite that hit the earth, causing the extinction of the dinosaurs and the age of the mammals.

Learning

Learning is the mechanism through which we can create permanent sustainable change, especially in behaviors. Learning can be self-driven, when you are actively reading, observing and thinking about your plans and consequences as you go through work and life experiences. It can be subliminal, when you do not realize you are learning. Once a creature experiences something it does not like, it is unlikely to repeat it. Sadly, humans as not as good at this as other creatures. Learning can also be propelled by the knowledge of others, through education, training, mentoring and supervised practice. Neither all theory nor all practice is as good as a balance of both. By itself, self-learning limits you to your own perspectives and interpretations, so a mix of kinds of learning works best.

Learning contributes to both development and evolution (see definitions above), but can happen only if the creatures want to learn. If they do not see any benefit to themselves, the learning activities do not have any lasting effect. (Ever tried to get a dog to do a new trick without a reward, or get your friends to help you with a project without some free beer or the offer of a dinner?)

A lot of learning happens in some Zoos, but unfortunately much is then lost because the creatures involved don't like what they have learned or fear sharing with other creatures because some may want all of the benefits for themselves. When the dog buries his bone, he tries to hide it from others, believing that all other dogs are doing the same.

To learn or put lessons into practice, we must often unlearn what we already know and change our own behavior to demonstrate that something different is actually possible. This is a capability that many creatures lack and that brings about the downfall of many Zoos.

One key element in learning effectiveness is the fun factor. People learn better if they are enjoying what they are doing. Too many education and or training programs are dry. People are bored to tears after the first five sentences and you lose them to last night's TV program or tomorrow's meeting. We need to make our learning programs more interactive and experience-based for better retention. Fun lessons are more likely to be retained and more likely to generate longer-term behavioral changes.

Microbiological

Without attention to minute details, a Zoo can decay through the destructive side effects of the creatures and the relationships among them. Everyone must actively monitor their Zoo and the creatures therein or you could all pay dearly.

Mood

Mood is a very interesting phenomenon affecting all creatures. It results in apparent inconsistencies in behaviors that make reading the creature a work of probability rather than one of pure science. Not taking mood into account lands you in trouble, regardless of the type of creature you are dealing with. What was taken as a joke yesterday gets your head bitten off today, simply because the creature is in a different mood. Don't confuse this with different creatures or mixed personalities. We all have up days and down days, and this does not make us different creatures. It is just a different behavior within our character profile range.

Human children very quickly come to understand this, and learn when to attempt requests and when not to. They usually ask a "mood tester" question first to determine the state of the parent and then, if they appear receptive, will then ask what they really want.

Perspective

Perspective is how you sense the world to be, from what you see, hear, smell, taste and feel. The trap with perception is that we think it is reality, but we can all perceive the same thing differently (see Reality below). Not only do we receive the sense signals differently, we interpret them differently because we each relate them to different experiences. So everything we perceive is actually a filtered and biased view of reality unique to ourselves, influenced by our culture and experiences. If there is a "true reality," a purely factual description of how the world truly is, we are not capable of fully describing it, because all signals pass through our inherently biased own perception.

Surviving in any corporate Zoo depends on how well you understand the balance between reality and perspectives and how well these two criteria are in balance with each other in your zoo. If your reality is a long way off from the common perspective of the corporate culture, you are not going to be happy or prosper in that environment. Remember, what is reality to you is just someone else's perspective to others. This does not mean that you are wrong! Rather, others do not see that you are right. Or you may have been right in the past, when things were different, but your position may not be right now (although it could be again in future).

Perspectives change all the time as does our world and our zoos. People throughout history have been burned at the stake or executed for suggesting something that was so ridiculous, it took hundreds of years before it became reality to the masses. Being a prophet (alias change agent), is an exciting career, but remember that most are worshiped only posthumously.

Whenever you hear "Get a grip," it is a good indication that your perspective (or reality?) is too far removed from accepted behaviors for the culture to tolerate. At this stage you have a decision to make: "fit in or flock off with others of your mindset."

Political Correctness

One of the more interesting evolutions of Western society in recent times is the pervasive campaign for political correctness. A lot of what most people would have found funny in the past is now taboo. We cannot be seen to find anything funny that relates to a specific religion, race, gender, sexual preference, belief, set of values or anything to do with a minority group or practice. In many countries, these requirements have been established in law.

So where does that leave those of us with a sense of humor? We have to throw out ninety percent of our old joke collections in case we insult someone. Yet many people still secretly find the old jokes funny, but they can't admit to it - at least in public.

In the heat of the moment, it is not the intent of the joker that matters. The reaction of the "target" determines the acceptability or inappropriateness of the joke. The issue is that the joker cannot predict how something as complex as a human will react in every circumstance. Reactions of the recipient will depend upon context and timing, presence or absence of others, their state of mind and their relationship with the joker. For these reasons we have all become more conservative in our fun jibes with others, and as a result, we laugh less. Some would argue that this is the necessary price of ensuring that we don't treat others with disrespect. I wish some sensible balance would be restored, so that we all had a little more (harmless) fun.

Imagine how much better off we would be if we could have a good old laugh at someone who did something silly without creating offense. Imagine how much happier the victim of the situation would be, too, if they had sufficient humor to be able to join in the laugh. Maybe they would feel a little embarrassed, but learning from their error in a fun way over a chuckle with friends seems a better option than losing friends because of overreacting and feeling insulted.

Many jokes are humorous because of a predictable behavior being driven by a particular set of characteristics. We find the joke funny because the outcome seems to be typical of a certain type of person. The problem we now have is that we (appropriately) cannot tell jokes about any particular type of people. So what do we do? Stop telling jokes? I hope not, as this will result in less laughter, and science shows that people who laugh a lot get ill less often and live longer. This of course assumes that they have not been laughing at someone powerful who lacks a sense of humor, in which case they simply disappear. The solution is of course to replace significant parts of large egos with a sense of humor, and then the subject has the capability to laugh with the situation instead of feeling they are being laughed at.

Despite this, there is a need for some degree of political sensitivity. It is simply not fair for certain people to be constant victims of targeted insults, as has happened in the past.

I propose that instead of telling jokes about a particular race, religion or minority group, we should tell jokes about creatures. Creatures (unlike humans) take a good joke on the chin and have a chuckle about it. They realize that they are true to their behavioral profile and would actually behave in the way suggested in the punch line. We can convert our race-based jokes (or those using any other bias) into creature-based jokes to preserve the humor without hurting the feelings of any particular human minority. For example, below is a joke that was originally based on one race being less intelligent than two others and is renovated with creatures instead.

A lion, a dog and a yak were walking past the Olympic stadium while a new stand was being constructed. They noticed there was an athletes' training session going on with some rather spectacular creature bodies on display, so they should take a closer look. They approached the gate and saw a guard and a sign saying "Athletes Only."

The lion quickly sized up the situation, picked up a crowbar from the construction site and confidently walked up to the guard. He proudly held up the crowbar and stated, "Here to practice my javelin." The guard nodded and the lion passed through to ogle at the athletes.

Seeing this, the dog quickly surveyed the surroundings and noticed some scaffolding materials. He picked up one of the bars and bounded past the guard calling "Pole vault" as he went into the stadium to enjoy the scenery.

The yak had to contemplate his chances for a while until he noticed a pile of posts and wire mesh leftover from the construction of a safety barrier. He happily grabbed a roll of wire, marched up to the guard and stated, "Fencing practice."

Reality

Reality is the pure, true, factual description of the world (or any situation or event). Put simply, reality is what is actually out there. But how do we know what this is when we can't agree? For most people, reality is what they believe to be the case, but in my reality at least, this is only a perspective (see Perspective above).

Sometimes your own reality can become distorted and can be quite different from what other people perceive the situation to be and what they see needs to happen as a result. The generally accepted reality in most Zoos is based on what the zookeeper decides is reality rather than what the majority believes to be the truth. This covers everything from acceptable behaviors to financial targets. Sometimes reality and fantasy get confused in the zookeeper's mind, and the rest of the creatures become a bit like the villagers in the story "The Emperor's New Clothes," letting him believe they all agree when in fact no one does. So reality becomes a relative thing. It depends upon who you are and what circumstances you are in.

Sense

Creatures react to what they sense more than to what they think. Humans like to believe they are the opposite, but this is a long way from the truth. Humans are highly advanced, but still creatures, and as such, reacting to how they subliminally sense a situation is still a major part of their behaviors.

Snails

You may not have noticed, but every picture in this book contains unobtrusive snails. (They're fun to find once you begin to look closely!) Yet there is no profile for them. This is because, while snails do exist in all organizations, no one really knows why they are there, or what purpose they serve. There are always more interesting things to gossip about than snails, aren't there?

Snails just slowly go about their own business in a (mostly) harmless manner and probably on balance contribute as much as they consume. They end up performing some menial tasks that no one else is prepared to take on, such as recycling the wastes. They are part of the food chain in some places so they also contribute to the overall balance of the environment, but they are more likely to meet their death simply by being in the wrong place at the wrong time, crushed by a bypasser who did not even notice them.

Transformation

As yet, this is an unproven theory that one species can evolve from another. Does an eagle have to be born an eagle, or can another creature learn all the traits of an eagle and adapt into one? The science of evolution argues that given sufficient time and environmental pressures new species are generated through adaptations from previous species, but this takes generations to occur.

So can a human leader be developed from a much simpler and less capable child, or are leaders born and their true characteristics just take time to become visible? Is your destiny decided by your genes, or can you manipulate your environmental conditions and develop your capabilities through a succession of different creatures to reach the top of the food chain? My answer is that both alternatives are right. Whichever you believe is right will happen, and you will create your own proof of your belief.

Virtual

In the human world Zoos are rapidly becoming less bound by physical barriers. Humans have evolved to the point where we can communicate with the other side of the world at the speed of light and maintain relationships with other people that we never get to meet physically.

This lays the foundation for a whole new kind of Zoo that we still have a lot to learn from. Traditionally physical barriers have served as the means to separate creatures from each other as well as to confine several in one space. Think of how we use cages, and then relate this to cubicles, office partitions, meeting rooms and offices. Organizations, like Zoos, have evolved to become more of an "open plains" style, and this has offered a host of advantages as well as a new set of complications to be managed.

In the new virtual business world, no such barriers exist anymore. There is no reason to confine your presence to one Zoo, as you can be a remote resident of any of a number of virtual Zoos around the world. Intranets and the Internet make possible new virtual relationships and great new opportunities to form new sorts of partnerships. The rules of engagement and the mechanisms of participation now require a whole new set of characteristics. However, proximity still is the best situation for learning and understanding, so as you go forth into new virtual environments, understand the food chain before you wander too widely, as wherever there is opportunity there are always both predators and prey.

On the positive side, though, is the opportunity to craft a virtual Zoo that is exactly to your liking. You can select the exact creatures you want to have in the Zoo. Without barriers and only agreed-upon constraints among the voluntary participants, the potential benefits are mind-boggling. Imagine your own little Zoo that you can totally control and no crowds to please, only like-minded creatures who want to develop an ongoing partnership. This is a somewhat idealistic perspective, I admit, but it is now possible. In most instances, virtual teams have a clear purpose that creates some value to someone, or they cease to attract participation.

Virus

A virus is a very simple type of organism that can infect other creatures. Generally they are quite harmful, and often reduce the performance capabilities, change the characteristics of, or even lead to the death of the host they infect. However, in rare cases, viruses contribute positive characteristics. Examples of this include causing the color variations in tulips, making them more beautiful, passing desirable genes (such as antibiotic resistance) to other individuals or even killing off or controlling an undesirable pest.

Common negative viruses in organizational Zoos include the *Paranoia virus*, the *Political virus* and the *Lying virus*. All of these are highly contagious and can easily pass from species to species very quickly. If a Zoo is infected by any of these, it rapidly becomes unhealthy and performs badly. Viruses are very difficult to treat, so constant vigilance must be applied to prevent infection. Once a Zoo is infected with one virus, it is more susceptible to secondary infections as well. This can complicate the symptoms and further drains energy from the Zoo. A common virus found in secondary infections is the *Highstaffturnover virus*. Once you have this very nasty virus, your Zoo needs to be admitted into intensive care and you must commit to a long and difficult recovery cycle.

Persistent infections of negative viruses can lead to a greater susceptibility to the *CYAatallcost virus*. This virus makes creatures more irritable and more aggressive (like the symptoms displayed in rabid dogs). Symptom-displaying *CYAatallcost virus* infections are not common, as the virus is often latent. However, under conditions of great stress, the symptoms suddenly appear and can cause deep, permanent consequences.

Positive viruses are less common and rarely found in poorly managed Zoos. However, in good Zoos, you can find simultaneous infections of the *Trust* virus and the *Honesty* virus. Infections with these two viruses often increase resistance to the negative viruses and increase the susceptibility to the *Happiness virus.* You can tell when you have these infections through the common symptom of smiles.

Another positive virus that can really enhance performance of the Zoo is the *Passion virus.* This virus, unlike many others, is more species specific and is not highly infectious. However, if you have a carrier or there is a long-term persistent infection of key individuals and their symptoms are obviously visible to others, it can gradually infect more individuals in the Zoo. You can increase susceptibility to the *Passion virus* by deliberately spreading the *Commitment virus.* You will find, though, that the *Commitment virus* needs constant reinfection as seasons change.

Vision

Having a vision for the future is a great thing, especially if you have the ability to share it with others and the capability and resources to bring about the vision. A creature with the characteristics to create such a vision, along with the drive and the influence to be able to deliver it is a rare beast indeed. There are far more visions than there are realities, but with a lot of effort, the right support and a great deal of time, the right vision can be realized. Sometimes this comes only after some near-disastrous attempts as we learn from the wrong paths we take along the journey. Occasionally we adjust the vision and improve upon it as a result of some of these wayward deviations and at other times, we realize that the original vision was fundamentally flawed. In that case, what appears to be a wrong turn may end up being a fortuitous change of direction.

For those deluded enough to think they can make a significant difference to the culture and behaviors of the Zoo as agenda item one on the heavily populated "To do tomorrow" list. I suggest some rethought. First reread the paragraphs on Vision and Behavior. Second, reread the rest of the book and consider what you need to make the difference. Ask yourself why anyone should support your change objective and follow your lead in this pursuit.

To significantly change your Zoo, you must enlist the support of the rest of its residents. Most creatures don't change easily. Motivating them to do so means curing the ubiquitously chronic disease of "don't care and don't want to."

A great vision and the charisma to influence others to follow you cure this problem. Just make sure that you are the right creature to carry it forward and that you enlist those who buy into your vision, as you will need their help.

Zoological

This is often an oxymoron, as there is very little logic that applies in many Zoos. There are of course some rules that do apply in Zoos with the right balanced hierarchy, but in many, logic goes out the window and the balance is lost. For example, we often see sloths as zookeepers, which very quickly destroys the whole balance. The Zoo becomes extinct to the peril of many creatures.

Last Thoughts

Can't decide which creature you are? Most humans are somewhat variable in their nature, and you can probably see some of yourself in many of the creature profiles. How you behave often highly depends on the situation and who else is present.

Also, other behaviors are inevitable as this book describes common profiles but can't possibly cover all of the combinations of characteristics you encounter in a Zoo. Hybrids occur in nature as well. Think of the characteristics of the bizarre platypus — a duckbilled, egg-laying mammal that lives in burrows under the water! You'd think this is completely absurd and must be unique (and it is), but other similarly ridiculous examples also exist. The echidna has a back entirely covered in spikes and lives in terrestrial burrows and eats only ants! The 25 profiles selected here are those you are most likely to encounter in everyday life.

You could well be a hybrid of characteristics from more than two creatures or in fact have a multiple creature complex. This is certainly the case for myself. I have some schizophrenic days where I bounce between different creatures, but then have other days where I remain in one creature mode.

Some will discover they are different creatures with different people (or are they a chameleon?), perhaps a sloth at home and an eagle at work, or vice versa in the case of the raving renovator. What creature you choose to be depends on the situation, the other creatures involved, and the environment. Your creature "mode" often depends on whether you feel you have the upper hand. Whether you become predator or prey, friend or foe, communal or solitary, can be outside your hands and very environmentally dependent. Ever tried to get rid of the relatives or find someone to help you move house? Sometimes you have more than you want and other times you can't get what you need.

In stressful situations you soon find out what you really are, as you tend to go back to your strongest creature type: mouse or lion? vulture or bee? eagle or sloth? Ultimately it is about choice and control. The more you are aware of yourself and your own creature idiosyncrasies, the more control you have and the better you are likely to react. Better decisions lead to better performance and ultimately enable you to become a more reliable, consistent and better creature. With such a positive spiral, you will be in a position to enjoy life and add value to other lives.

Humor

I trust that this is not the only place that you will find humor in this book, but at least I can honestly market the book as containing humor now! After all, it has a whole section dedicated to the subject!

This book is designed to encourage you to explore and experiment with interpersonal relationships in a fun way. Maybe you can have a laugh at some of the characteristics of others as well as laugh at yourself occasionally. If more of us could do this, it would be a much better world. Using the creatures and a dose of humor allows you to approach what can be a very serious problem with a less than serious perspective. The removal of personal references and the addition of a few smiles will greatly increase the chances of resolving problems as well.

It may appear that the author is very negative about consultants and people who have completed MBA's. However, this is not completely true. Some of the people the author most highly respects and admires are consultants with MBA's. It is not about these characteristics per se, it is the attitude that very often accompanies them. That is, "I am a consultant or I have an MBA, therefore I have the right to tell you what to do in your business as I know better than you."

Well, as someone with a sense of humor, no MBA but with reasonable experience (and having worked as a consultant myself), I know this is simply not true. Those with MBA's, an understanding of reality, respect for experience and a sense of humor will also know this. They realize their limitations and hopefully will see the humor in the book (or perhaps see the characteristics in others they work with, but not themselves).

You learn better if you have a sense of humor. The ability to laugh at mistakes you have made is a wonderful thing. First, it gets you to admit what you have done, and second, it allows you to share the lessons from this error with others. Hopefully, they will then not make the same mistake.

Some workplaces have instigated an award for the silliest mistake of the week or month. This has increased the communications between team members and generated a sense of fun in the office. The small investment of time to facilitate this has always added much more back in lessons and morale. Learning happens more effectively and provides better long-term outcomes if you are having fun when you do it.

I hope you can make some positive use of the book like this, but I also trust that you have enjoyed reading it just for fun as well. Keep smiling, and enjoy your new creature ways.

About the Author

Arthur Shelley lives in Melbourne, Australia, with his wife Joy and two daughters, Cathy and Helen. Although a microbiologist by education, he has spent the last ten years working on international business process change projects. Through this experience, he became aware of the importance of understanding and engaging people in organizations in order to influence them to achieve mutually acceptable outcomes. When he privately began adding creature metaphors to make the job more entertaining and remove some of the politics, interacting with others became much more fun and far less stressful.

About the Illustrator

John Szabo lives in Melbourne, Australia, with his wife Liz and three children, Stefanie, Tomas and Peter. An engineer by profession, John also has a creative artistic streak that finds him drawing cartoons and playing violin and saxophone. For the past ten years, he has been working on major IT and restructuring projects. Before which he managed planning and production engineering.

Visit
www.organizationalzoo.com
to send electronic profiles to friends
and see the latest Zoo events.

Surviving Breast Cancer

Retired pathologist, author, and breast cancer survivor, Deborah Douglas, M.D., walked 600 miles in 10 Breast Cancer 3-Day events to interview cancer survivors and co-survivors. The collected stories not only emphasize the complexity of diagnosis, treatment, and survivorship, but—due in large part to the emotional honesty of the contributors—challenge the popular mantras that a positive attitude is the only healthy way to cope with the disease and that cancer is an unequivocal gift.

Read this book if you are:

- A cancer patient or loved one who wants to know how other patients handle the challenges of diagnosis, treatment, and survivorship and still find the courage to participate in a long-distance walk

- A health-care provider who wants cancer patients to understand that there are no right or wrong ways to face this disease

- Interested in signing up for a Breast Cancer 3-Day event, but want to know what it's really like to walk 60 miles, sleep in a tent, shower in a truck, and use porta-potties

- Simply curious why an otherwise perfectly reasonable middle-aged woman would leave behind her comfortable home, family, friends, and dogs to walk 600 miles in 10 cities

The chapters deftly weave together incidents, observations, and conversations from the walks themselves; the stories of survivors and their families; the medical "journeys" of those survivors along with accessible technical explanations; and occasional incidents and insights from the author's own story. The writing is technically excellent, compassionate, humorous, and emotionally open. Everything about this book is exemplary.

—Dianne Schilling, Instructional Designer

ISBN: 0944031 24 2

www.AslanPublishing.com • www.the3-daybook.com
Available nationally at bookstores and online webstores

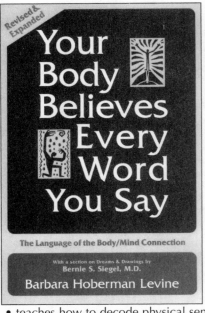